Hung Out to Dry
Swimming and British Culture

First Edition (XI)

© Christopher Robert Ayriss 2009, 2010, 2011, 2012

ISBN 978-0-557-12428-2

All rights reserved. Except for the purpose of review, no part of this book may be reproduced in any form or by any means, without the prior permission of the author.

Published by Lulu.com

Copies of this book may be purchased either direct from the publisher or from the author's website at:

www.hungouttodry.co.uk

Hung Out to Dry
Swimming and British Culture

Chris Ayriss

For Ann and my children

Front cover: 1926 Serpentine, Hyde Park, London.

Rear cover: St Ives, Cornwall.

Contents

Introduction · 7

1 From Pride to Prejudice · 11

2 Cleanliness versus Godliness · 39

3 Sex, Sea and Swimming Trunks · 55

4 Sunny Days, Dark Shadows · 75

5 Lidos Open, Rivers Close · 91

6 Leicester: Swim City · 115

7 The Last Stand · 141

Credits · 153

Index · 154

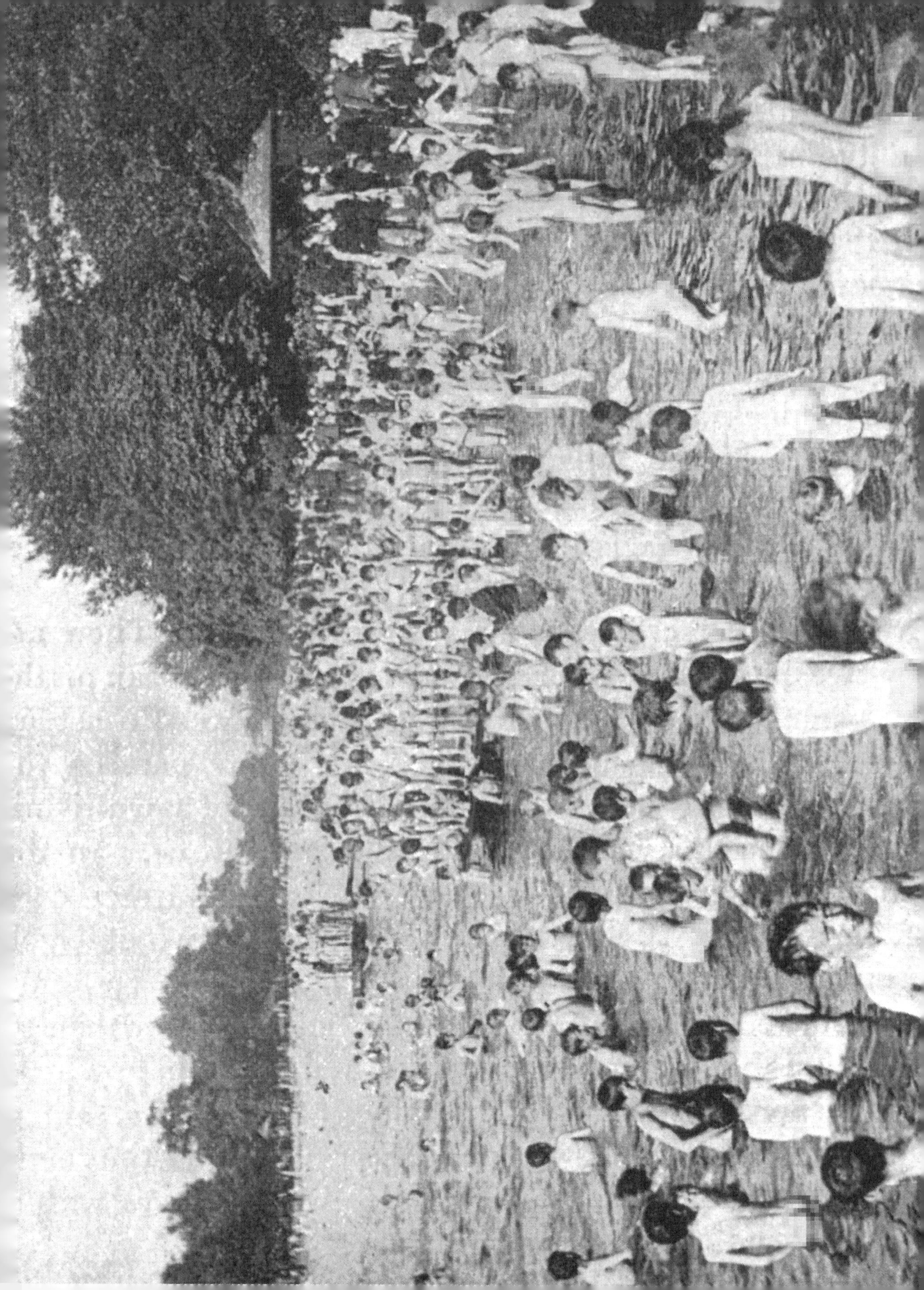

Introduction

Growing up in the baby boom generation, my friends and I enjoyed a freedom that most of today's youngsters are denied. The streets and parks swarmed with children and our love of the outdoors enriched our lives. Such liberty seems impossible today as child protection has cleared the streets, but in those days children wandered about everywhere and I discovered a great deal while enjoying my freedom. Every now and then I would cycle past Leicester's old bathing station and read the large painted letters: 'For swimming only.' Chain hand rails reach along the canal-side as a haunting reminder of the popularity of this place. On one side of the canal swimming was obviously encouraged, but then on the other side stood a warning: 'DO NOT BATHE!' Why had the Corporation built a swimming pool into the canal if the water was unfit for bathing? If the water was unfit, why were the children that swam in it so healthy? No one seemed to have any answers and so began my quest to unravel the puzzle for myself and a journey that has taken me all over the country.

The publication of this book resulted from another discovery made years later whilst walking with my wife along the canal bank. We came across a police notice asking for the public's assistance in preventing crime on the waterside.[1] The appeal was for witnesses to anti-social behaviour like vandalism and motorcycle use and this I could understand. But the list of offences included children seen swimming in the canal and such 'criminals' were to be reported in

Opposite: The Bathing Lake, Victoria Park, London. Described by Lieutenant-Colonel Sexby as foremost among the park's facilities! 'As many as 25,000 bathers have been counted on a summer's morning.' The lake was open to swimmers between 4.00-8.00 a.m. in the summer; the early hours ensured that the working day was not impeded. Sexby continues: 'What an incalculable boon open air swimming-baths like those provided here must prove to the neighbourhood! The principle bathing-lake is 300 feet long. It is provided with a concrete bottom, shelters, and diving-boards, and all the accessories to make it a perfect out-door swimming-bath, and it has been pronounced the finest in the world. In case of accidents, two boatmen are always on duty during the season, which is a necessary precaution when the number of bathers is taken into account.' Nearby a play park and a sand pit were well maintained despite the high costs in order to brighten the lives of local children. The park was used by swimmers from 1846.

---

[1] Leicester summer 2007.

just the same way as a mugger or a thief, by dialling 999. For my part I had not considered swimming to be a criminal offence, certainly not on a level with motorcycling through crowds of unsuspecting walkers on the towpath. Nor could I see swimming in the same bracket as mindless vandalism. Yet at the bottom of this notice the caption was clear: 'getting personal with criminals!' You might think that child protection is at the root of this criminalization of childish joys. Perhaps fears about pollution are putting us off enjoying the water in the sunshine. Yet our rivers are the cleanest they have ever been. Why then do we still feel as though river swimming must be wrong? A child might of course drown, yet that does not stop us letting children swim in the sea. What then is so different about swimming in canals, rivers and lakes?

As I began my research into the British swimmer I was shocked to discover that public swimming had meant nudity for all. Illustrated on page 6 is one of many old photographs that picture children bathing. As you can see, it was once incredibly popular; but why was it only boys that swam? More puzzling still is their lack of costume and embarrassment. Such pictures expose a very different Britain to that of today. How we British have changed! Just imagine the reaction such scenes would cause these days! Looking further I discovered that our changing attitudes toward nudity underpinned the prejudice that has developed towards the swimmer. We accept that attitudes evolve with time. Yet we British have changed completely from accepting total nudity for swimming, to viewing such as perverse or even kinky today.

Over the years it has taken me to compile this book, attitudes have dramatically changed. Today fears for the safety of children have completely reshaped our culture. Who would have thought that even parents would eventually be excluded from school sports days so as to protect children from predators? Yet it would seem that we have thrown out the baby with the bathwater. Parents and children are now paranoid about safety, yet at the same time whole sections of our bookshops are devoted to child abuse accounts. The nation has developed a thirst for lurid details of inappropriate intimacy and children are in effect abused twice over as their 'dirty linen' is aired in public. Daily, newspapers rob them of dignity by poring over the details of such scandals, and the internet fuels the problem making child exploitation all too easy. So, as the nation has become obsessed with stranger danger, opportunities for paedophiles to fan their desires are proliferating. As important as it is to protect trusting children from exploiters, you will discover that the vast majority of abuse stems from an entirely different source, in effect we are stopping up the draught around the window whilst leaving the door wide open! Feelings naturally run high on this topic and so I have decided in this revision to censure some of the illustrations. It is hoped that with this revision all readers will be able to look at these images without embarrassment. Each picture appears for a reason, with this modification I trust that all will be able to look beyond the undressed state of early swimmers, to focus on the message that each print conveys. This book covers far more than the history of British swimming; it explores the link between swimming and changes in British culture that reach into our individual daily lives. Without these photographs, the true magnitude of the social changes we British have experienced cannot be fully appreciated; they provide a window onto our past, revealing the extent to which swimming has influenced British culture. If you want to understand what has made the British what they are, you are holding the answer in your hands!

Our way of life is unique; we are branded with a smutty sense of humour and we display a fascination for nudity in newspapers and magazines. Yet at the same time we are uncomfortable with exposure in even the most natural of settings. Take for example a new mother that nurses her infant in public. The British reaction of embarrassment moves the 'offender' to feel self-conscious, and in future to feed out of sight for the sake of 'decency'. How did we come to develop such attitudes? Through this book you will come to see just how dramatically the culture of our nation has changed, and how we have subtly influenced the customs of other peoples. It exposes the underlying reason for the prejudice shown towards swimming in the great outdoors and in the first chapter you will see how the attitudes of our nation have transformed beyond recognition in the last hundred years. The revelations contained herein will show how and why the British people, once proud of their swimming heritage, developed their prejudice towards swimmers. To begin with let us look at the history of swimming, its rise to popularity and its fall from grace.

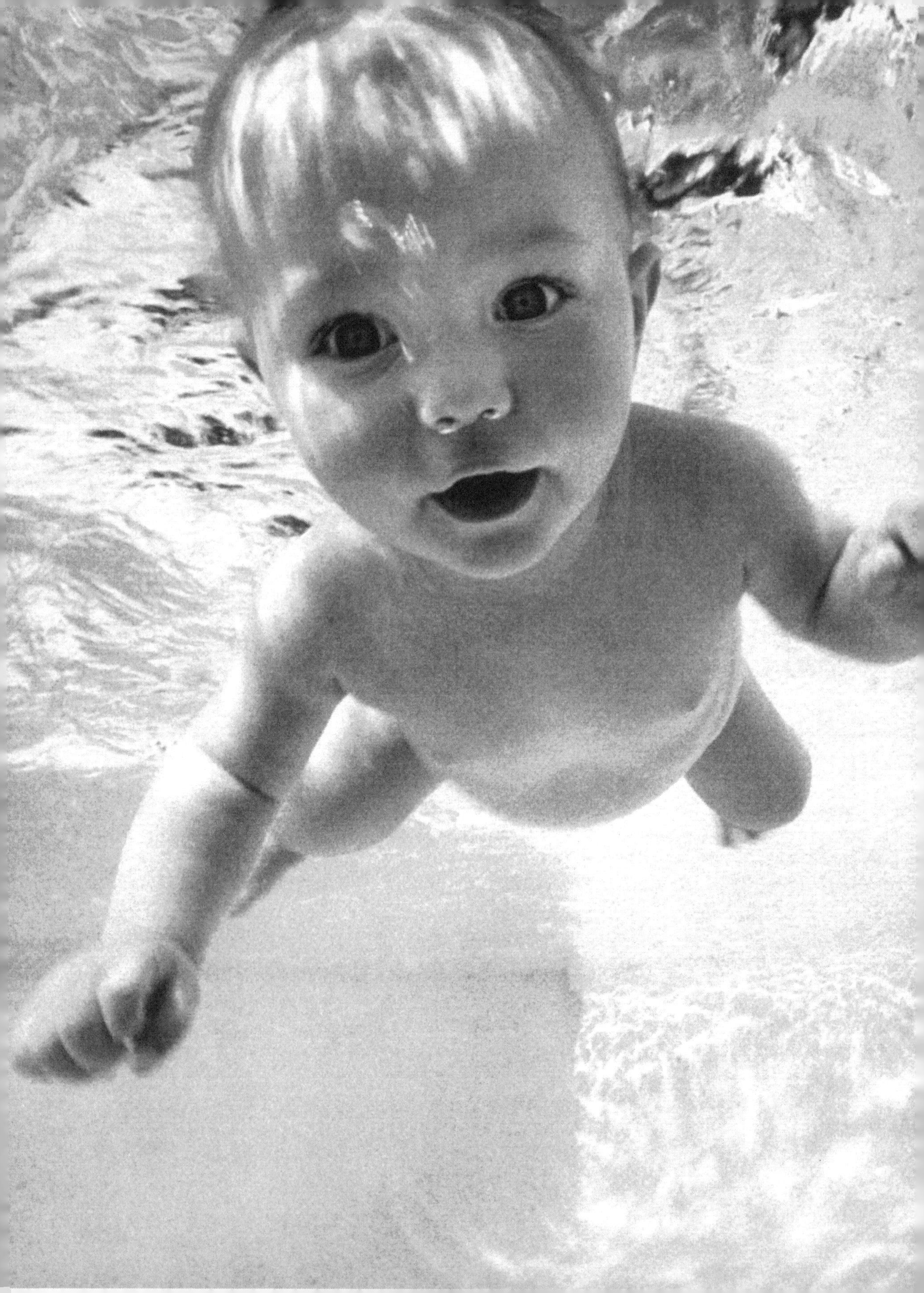

Chapter 1
From Pride to Prejudice

Dusting off the Past

A newborn baby is held by the midwife, and gently lowered feet first onto the bed. Without hesitation, this tiny infant begins to move her legs in a reflex action that makes it look as though she is walking. It will of course be several months before she can actually support her own weight. Surprisingly though, when submerged, a similar reflex causes a baby to close her mouth and move her tiny arms and legs in such a way that they propel the delighted swimmer along. As with walking, swimming still has to be learnt, so it comes as no surprise that one of the first historic references to swimming is an early Egyptian text, wherein a father mentions his children's swimming lessons. Water was very important to the Egyptians. Their ancient priests purified themselves each morning by bathing in the sacred waters of the Nile and it was whilst she was river-bathing that Pharaoh's daughter discovered Moses in a floating basket. The Egyptians viewed their river as a god, feeling the greatest tribute one could render to it was to be drowned in its flow, in fact the Egyptian word for drowned originally meant praise.

'An ignorant man neither knows how to read nor to swim.' This ancient proverb reveals just how the Romans esteemed swimming. Just as we frown on illiteracy today, they looked down on non-swimmers as incompetent. For the Romans the skill was essential. At a time when bridges were few, it often provided the only means for river crossing; an army that could swim was seen as unstoppable!

We might see the leisure pool as a modern invention, but it's the Romans we have to thank for the luxury of heated swimming baths.[2] Written records of swimming in Britain start with the Romans and we find that Julius Caesar was himself an acclaimed swimmer; he famously escaped from the Egyptians at Alexandria by swimming to the safety of a nearby ship. The Romans bathed for both health and pleasure yet most of the baths they built were small, designed to pamper to the flesh, with facilities for sweating, washing and, of course, bathing. Swimming pools were rarely included with such accommodations as the river was seen as the swimmers' preferred habitat. How-

---

[2] Gaius Maecenas (70-8 BCE) is thought to have built the very first such pool.

Hung Out to Dry

ever, there were exceptions. The Empire furnished Britain with a number of swimming pools with the largest using the warm waters of Bath.[3] They can hardly be said to have set a trend though, as no more pools were built until the Industrial Revolution.

Today we read to our infants, aware of their tremendous potential to learn, likewise the Romans were quick to introduce their young to the water as the following excerpt shows: *'Strong from the cradle, of a sturdy brood, We bear our newborn infants to the flood; There bathed amid the stream our boys we hold, with winter hardened and inured to cold.'* [4] Children's lives were at stake; parents could not afford to be casual about such education. Rush floats were used to assist early learners and river swimming was very much encouraged; the cold waters of the Tiber were especially popular despite there being eight hundred and fifty public baths in Rome.

Assyrian fugitives escape by swimming on inflated animal skins. They were evidently caught by surprise as they are fully dressed. The swimmer at the top has been shot by an arrow, yet he swims unaided against the current and appears to be using the front crawl.

---

[3] Others have been discovered at Chester, Exeter, Wroxeter, Caerleon and Gadebridge. It is thought that Buxton may also have been blessed with a large pool. Sadly the remains were covered over in the 1780s by the building of the Crescent and as there are no detailed records regarding the Roman structure, it is impossible to say for certain.
[4] Dryden: *Ninth book of Virgil's Aeneid*, Numanus taunting the Trojans.

From Pride to Prejudice

Assyrians soldiers depicted crossing a river in traditional swimming apparel - au naturel.

Excavations revealed just how extensive such facilities were. Picture a building similar in size to the Houses of Parliament,[5] imagine gymnasia lecture halls and hot rooms all circling a gigantic swimming pool; this is Caracalla. The baths opened at eight in winter, with relaxation and pleasure being the key elements of the visit. Most patrons did not arrive until around noon, after which they spent the rest of the day pampering their flesh. Exclusivity is a requirement for many of today's health clubs, but not so in Rome. All could afford to enjoy this inexpensive pleasure and so the baths came to be something of a national obsession.

History shows that bathing has always been a social affair; people prefer to bathe with companions and thus bathing places became established social centres. The same holds true on the riverbank with swimmers congregating at well-established swimming holes. In the early days men and women bathed separately, but as time passed mixed bathing became popular indoors and this

---

[5] The baths covered an area of 28 acres and could accommodate 1,600 bathers.

led to a rise in the number of scandals related to the baths. Emperor Hadrian issued a decree to separate the sexes in the hope of restoring decency and this ruling coincided with the introduction of the baths to Britain.

As the Romans expanded their Empire, their bathing customs travelled with them. Soldiers would spend hours pampering their flesh, scraping their skin, being massaged with oil and having their body hair plucked. The provincial baths far from Rome saw enthusiastic young people push social limits to breaking point. Hadrian's separating the sexes may well have reduced the scandals surrounding mixed bathing, but it could do little to repress the rise in homosexual liaisons; in fact well-endowed males were often applauded as they entered the baths. The moral and social decline proved unstoppable. Attitudes deteriorated, ending in the downfall of the baths and moral decay. Originally, Roman males swam in frigid conditions, epitomising the prowess of the nation,[6] and swimming had enjoyed an elevated status, seen both as life-saving and health giving. Its value to the army was such that a soldier's being able to swim gave the military a fighting edge unequalled elsewhere. Swimming skill thus fulfilled the ideal.

Bath Time

So what of Britain? As elsewhere, swimming and bathing are inseparably linked. After all, don't we still refer to the swimming pool and swimming bath as one and the same thing? Take the city of Bath as an example. Famous around the world for its hot springs, yet renowned for its legendary Roman swimming pool. These waters, sacred to the Celts,[7] have been a bathing place from the dawn of history. A story that began more than eight hundred years before Christ, finds handsome Prince Bladud returning from his travels, smitten, alas, with leprosy. Unlike the prodigal son of the Bible, his father did not receive him with open arms, but rather at arms length, and put him under guard. Suitably disguised, he slipped away and began a new life in Swainswick as a swine herder. Things surely couldn't get much worse. Yet Bladud next jumps into some steaming mud and starts to wallow in it along with the pigs! Had he gone mad? Apparently not, he'd noticed that of all his pigs, those that rolled in the mud were free of sores. Having jumped into the mire, low and behold his leprosy vanished! Delighted to see his son cured, the King restored his inheritance, which ultimately led to his succeeding to the throne. Bladud became the ninth King of the Britons, and not forgetting his good fortune built the city of Caer

---

[6] *'Our hardy race brings its sons to the rivers early and hardens them to the waters'* (Virgil).
[7] Connecting them to their sun god Sul.

Baden (as Bath was formally known) around the springs, so that others could benefit from their healing powers.

Caer Baden excited the Romans when they invaded. Finding the ancient Celtic shrine to Sul at what is now known as the King's Bath (the source of the spring) they renamed the town Aquae Sulis. The ancient god Sul and the Roman goddess Minerva were merged into one; a temple was built and the complex expanded to include their own Roman style baths. A swimming pool and a theatre were also added to complement the original spa, which attracted visitors from across Europe. These exciting changes were completed by 75 AD and the baths remained in use until the late 4th Century. Bathing here was more than a sanitary exercise. Patrons would commune with the water spirit as they submerged, writing messages to her and dropping them down into the water, casting spells on those that had offended the bathers.

The temple and buildings fell into disrepair after the Romans left us, but it would appear that the spring was maintained to some degree, as the town was renamed by the Saxons as Akemanceaster or Sick Man's Town. Early in the 12th Century the monks of Bath refurbished the spring and renamed it as the King's Bath, after Henry 1st. Cubicles were carved into the walls providing privacy for the bathers, but inevitably this led to scandal. In 1559 it was decreed that anyone having reached puberty was required to wear a robe whilst bathing. Again this led to difficulties given that the robes of most were far from clean. However, the solution to the clean/moral dilemma and the sexes bathing together was resolved, when in 1576 an adjoining bath was built, namely the Queen's Bath. This, it was hoped, would accommodate propriety as well as answering Bishop Bubwith's objection to the sexes bathing together. Interestingly, at one time people were expected to remove all their clothing for hygienic reasons, facing a fine unless they bathed in the nude. The seesaw between morality and cleanliness thus found expression in the warm waters of Bath.[8]

Getting Our Feet Wet

As for the rest of the country, invasion by the Anglo Saxons led to the ruination of Roman Britain,[9] yet both sexes of these Germanic settlers were capable swimmers.[10] Pope Gregory I sent Augustine to reclaim the island as Christian

---

[8] The rediscovery of the old Roman baths began in 1727, when workmen discovered the gilded bronzed head of Minerva during excavations for a sewer trench. The large lead-lined swimming pool was discovered in 1880.
[9] The country was renamed Angle-Land or England. The various tribes held different areas; with the Angles holding Mercia (the Midlands), Northumbria and East Anglia.
[10] An Anglo Saxon word – 'Syndig' related to 'Sund' literally means: 'trained in swimming.'

Hung Out to Dry

following Rome's demise and the Angles were won over starting with the baptism of Æthelberht King of Kent. The old Roman Church at Canterbury was repaired and Augustine was made Archbishop. Then the Vikings invaded. Swimming was nothing out of the ordinary to them either, in fact they would have successfully wiped out Christianity and protected swimmers from the censure of Christendom had it not been for Alfred the Great, King of Wessex, who defeated the invaders' great army at Chippenham (878AD). The Danes signed a treaty agreeing to leave Wessex free and were subsequently baptised according to its terms. As it turned out this was more than a token gesture with many sincerely embracing the Christian faith.

The Norman Conquest brought heavily clad armed knights to our land; a knight's focus was certainly not towards swimming but was centred on chivalry.[11] Times had changed; whereas in the Roman era an army that could swim had a distinct advantage, now the horse proved to be a formidable weapon of war, allowing its rider to advance or retreat at great speed without having to rely on any ability to swim. The impracticality of swimming in armour, along with the influence of the Catholic Church, led to the discouragement of both swimming and bathing. Regular bathing had become uncommon even among the rich. Englishmen had little to do with water, in fact the feet of King Henry IV were said to be so unbelievably dirty that they *'stank to high heaven.'* There was a loathing for soap and water, eau-de-cologne being used instead. Queen Elizabeth of the 16th Century and her associates all used strong perfumes to cover up the pungent result of their ablutionary negligence, and considering that the British were so frightened of water there is little wonder that swimming was avoided. Across Europe people found body odour to be an attractive stimulant and long after bathing was reintroduced Napoleon wrote to Josephine: *'will be home in three weeks, **don't wash**.'*[12] With our preoccupation with cleanliness today, the idea of body odour might seem repulsive, but in times past things were very different. In fact *un-cleanliness* was seen as next to godliness, with the clean being perceived as partners with the Devil. The collapse of the Roman Empire began with the bath; bathing led to immorality and immorality to family breakdown and the destruction of the very fabric of society. This ultimately led to the disintegration of the Empire and so, bathing, seen as the cause of all these troubles, was to be avoided at all costs.

Youngsters, however, could not resist the water. Swimming later resurfaced in London as well as at Oxford and Cambridge Universities.[13] Sadly there

---

[11] Horsemanship.
[12] Married in 1796.
[13] Parsons Pleasure, Oxford, on the river Cherwell is mentioned in records as early as 1689.

were many accidents, moving the Vice Chancellor, John Whitgift to threaten that anyone caught swimming would be severely punished.[14] Undergraduates would be beaten for a first offence whereas a Bachelor of Arts was to be placed in the stocks for a day and fined ten shillings. Those that dared to swim again were expelled. But things were set to change; just sixteen years later Everard Digby published his work: *De Arte Natandi* (The art of swimming: 1587). Originally written in Latin, to elevate the status of swimming to that of an Art or a Science, he aimed to promote its virtues and reduce the number of those drowning at Cambridge. However, its readership was limited to the upper classes until its translation into English in 1595. Only then did Digby's work begin to have any real life saving effect, by improving swimming efficiency. Through his book, Digby held the prospective swimmer 'by the hand' explaining where it was safe to swim, how to enter the water, how to swim along and even surface dive. Advice was given not to swim alone and to limit one's adventures to the warmer months from May to August. An accompanying wood cut picture illustrated each aspect, which added greatly to its charm (Nicholas Orme: *Early British Swimming 55 BC-AD 1719*).

Every aspect of swimming was covered in Digby's book; here he illustrates circumvolution.

Swimming slowly became more prominent. William Shakespeare in his play *Henry VIII* has Cardinal Wolsey remark: '*I have ventured, like little wanton boys that swim on bladders, this many summers in a sea of glory, but far beyond my depth.*' Inflated bladders were a popular swimming aid that continued in use until the 20th Century

---

[14] Cambridge, May 1571.

Hung Out to Dry

despite their disadvantages. They putrefy in the water, becoming smelly and very unpleasant; little wonder the fairer sex found learning to swim unattractive.

Another early reference to swimming involves Colonel Blood and his arrest in 1671 for stealing the Crown Jewels. In his confession to King Charles II he explained that he'd previously been *'engaged to shoot his Majesty as he* **went to swim** *in the Thames above Battersea, but that when he was about to take aim, the awe of Majesty paralysed his hand, and that he not only gave up his design but bound his confederates to do the same.'*[15] Thus the King is seen as no stranger to the sport, a fact likely adding much to its acceptability.

Doctor Knows Best

Britain's spas had by now begun to attract visitors from abroad. They depended largely on patronage by the rich, to offset the steady stream of poor bathers hoping to cure illnesses and injuries. Then Dr Wittie of Scarborough recommended a revolutionary idea. Scientists accepted that spring water cured the sickly; so surely then seawater could hold benefits for the ill. From 1667 this new source of medicine was used both internally and externally as a health cure.

Cold bathing in seawater went on to become very popular as a treatment for even the most stubborn of diseases. With the success of such treatments, doctors enjoyed a newfound credibility. This they exploited, by recommending all kinds of other treatments as being similarly effective. However Sir John Floyer was not at all happy with this. He deplored the way that the cold water cure was being abandoned in favour of other treatments. He said in effect that the departure from such natural cures was due to a desire on the part of the medical profession to exploit more fantastic and more profitable methods of dealing with disease. Yet cold water was seen to have other advantages as expressed in the following recommendation:[16]

'Cold Bathing has this good alone,
It makes old John to hug old Joan!
And gives a sort of Resurrection,
To bury'd joy's throu' lost Erection,
And does fresh kindnesses entail,
On a wife tasteless, old and stale.

---

[15] Sinclair & Henry: *Swimming, The Badminton Library* 1893.
[16] Floyer and Baynard: *The history of cold bathing* 1720.

Advantages indeed! With such regenerative properties, cold water put new life into the elderly, attracting many to the dawn swim throughout the country as a natural and inexpensive forerunner of the drugs available today.

The cold bath was also used to strengthen weak children and this it did, although some were over-zealous in their efforts to restore the sickly, as well as being unrealistic in their expectations. Children of course have always enjoyed experimenting with, and paddling in, cold water however dirty it might be, as the following reference from 1728 shows:

> *To where fleet-ditch with disemboguing streams*
> *Rolls the large tribute of dead dogs to Thames,*
> *The King of Dykes!*
>
> *Than whom no sluice of mud,*
> *With deeper sable blots the silver flood.*
>
> *'Here strip my children! Here at once leap in,*
> *Here prove who best can dash through thick and thin,*
> *And the most in love of dirt excel*
> *Or dark dexterity of groping well'*[17]

Thus the health benefits generated by coldwater bathing meant that Britain's spas enjoyed a rebirth.

Moral Dangers

As bathing increased in popularity, eyebrows were being raised and concerns vocalised about the moral dangers to which eager bathers were being exposed. Regardless of what went on or off by the sea or on the riverbank, propriety had to be observed indoors. The Corporation of Bath became so worried about public morality, that in 1737 they insisted: *'no male person over ten years was to bathe without a pair of drawers and a waistcoat and no female person without a decent shift.'* Chapter three deals with the development of swimming costumes in more detail, but it is interesting to note that even before this, the feeling that costumes ought to be worn was expressed in Daniel Defoe's book: *Robinson Crusoe*, of 1719. The shipwrecked islander prepares to swim back to the wreck intending to salvage what he can, and yet, despite the fact that he is entirely alone he swims wearing breeches![18] As more and more bathers flocked

---

[17] Dunciad, (Barton: *The Lost Rivers of London* 1962).
[18] His covering set him apart from the savages and elevated him and his nation as superior.

to the coast, nudity was to be seen everywhere. To preserve modesty at the seaside, a Quaker, Benjamin Beal, presented his brand new invention - the Bathing Machine - on Margate Sands in 1753. Even so bathers were still seen to be at risk, so much so that when another new development surfaced many expressed the view that washing could now be abandoned. 'Undergarments' it was said 'made bathing quite unnecessary,' but not everyone agreed and the opposite view was preserved for us in the *Gentleman's Magazine of 1769*:

> *'The ancients were more neat than we are. Their daily and continual bathing and those currycombs with which they scraped their bodies, some of which are still preserved, kept them always clean and did not leave any dirt on the skin. Our shirts cannot answer the same purpose, however careful we may be to change them often. This is evident: for not withstanding the frequent shifting of our linen, we still collect filth, which can only be removed by water and bathing.'*

Ridicule was thus poured on the notion that the wearing of undergarments made bathing redundant.

The Seaside Fashion

In time the spa at Bath began to lose its popularity and especially so as the Prince of Wales travelled along with King George III to Brighthelmstone to bathe. From its insignificant beginnings in the 1780s Brighton (as it is now known) was thus born as the sea-bathing capital. It became King George IV's second home and so, as we might expect, sea bathing now came firmly into fashion.

People seemed to have been much hardier in those early bathing days. In her diary, Madame D'Arblay mentions bathing at Brighton in 1782, notice the date!

> *'Wednesday **November 20th**. Mrs and the three Miss Thrales and myself all rose at six o'clock in the morning and by the pale blink of the moon we went to the seaside, whence we had bespoke the bathing–women be ready for us and into the ocean we plunged. It was cold, but pleasant. I had bathed so often as to lose my dread of the operation, which now gives me nothing but animation and vigour.'*

Can you imagine today, rising so early and at such a cold time of year just to bathe in the ocean? Of course the benefits we could get from bathing remain, but most are simply put off by the cold and so never experience its pleasures.

Swimming Captivates the Nation

For those that actually swam, the breaststroke was the most commonly used means of propulsion. The *Encyclopaedia Britannica* of 1797 advised that a frog should be kept in a tub of water as a natural demonstration of the stroke, and many learned by such imitation. They would lie prone, supported on a chair moving their limbs in the air, encouraged by their little instructor. When speed was required swimmers generally used the sidestroke. So as Nelson gained mastery of the seas, winning victory on the Nile in 1798 and at Trafalgar in 1805, Britons back home began to pride themselves on their accomplishments as swimmers.

The British became world famous for their fascination with swimming and bathing. Many experimented with long distance swims and the development of endurance. Lord Byron[19] swam the Hellespont and went on to write:

> *'I plume myself on this achievement more than I could possibly do any kind of glory, political, poetical, or rhetorical.'*

Byron recorded in his poetry the thrilling sensations of swimming. He delighted in the sea and he felt a buoyancy of spirits after each encounter. In Europe such eccentrics, who would bathe in even the coldest of conditions, were met with outright disbelief. But even so, the swimming tradition of the British went on to lead the world into a new association with water. Due to its unique position, the British Empire set the fashion as swimming capital of the world. The British took pride in their swimming supremacy, Britain ruled the waves; the world looked on in awe and began to copy its example.

It is thought that the first indoor bath built and advertised as a place to swim (since Roman times) was a bagnio in London (May 28 1742).[20] The outdoor Peerless pool opened a year later in Finsbury; with Clifton Lido, Bristol, being the oldest post-Roman pool (opened in July 1850) in use today.

Diving was to become a very popular spectator sport. Samuel Scott, for example, attracted great crowds on his visit from America, with such feats as diving from the cliff at Portreath in Cornwall. Although the cliff rises some two hundred and forty feet, he would plunge into just eight feet of water! One arm of the harbour reaches out around the cliff providing an ideal vantage point for spectators (the launching point is still accessible today and although the art of diving into such shallow water has now all but disappeared, children still regularly jump into the sea here at high tide). Displays like this were commonly

---

[19] 1788 – 1824.
[20] Lemon Street, Goodman's Fields.

staged from seaside piers, as well as from the bridges of London. Each provided the perfect venue for dare devil divers to perform their stunts, and crowds came to see the excitement.[21]

A new development for those in England, at least, was the discovery in 1844 of the front crawl and this caused something of a sensation. *The Times* reported on the race between two North American Red Indians namely Tobacco and Flying Gull and the English man Harold Kenworthy. Kenworthy of course used the traditional English breaststroke. The Red Indians failed to impress:

> *'Their style of swimming is totally un-European. They lash the water violently with their arms like the sails of a windmill and beat downward with their feet, blowing with force and performing grotesque antics.'*

Despite the fact that this stroke had been used for centuries in more tropical climes, it seemed that no one had taken any notice of it. Kenworthy won the race and so Britons persevered with the breaststroke for another thirty years.

Also in 1844, the move towards providing bathing and washing opportunities for the working classes led to the formation of the 'Association for Promoting Cleanliness among the Poor.' This led in turn to the building of a bathhouse and laundry in Glasshouse Street, East Smithfield. Its success caused the 1846 'Public Bath and Wash Houses Act' to be passed, but the accommodations this Act afforded were not very popular, as it provided for only the very poorest sections of the community. The baths it made available were perceived as being on a level with the Workhouse, but provision for swimmers lay just around the corner.

In January 1849, London's premier swimming baths were opened at St Martins-in-the-Fields, just off Leicester Square. Its success led to rapid development and within just three years, London could boast seven swimming baths in total, to which 800,000 bathers were attracted annually. By 1861 Turkish baths were springing up everywhere, which well suited the richer public, who delighted in their exclusivity.

At this time of intense interest in swimming, a great number of devices were patented, which budding inventors hoped would not only aid swimming efficiency, but also earn them their fortune. Some were intended to teach students the art of swimming; others were designed to increase speed. None proved to be of any lasting benefit despite exaggerated claims. Their failure was predictable, as swimming does not in any way lend itself to cumbersome restrictions that inhibit free and natural movement. Experiments abounded. In

---

[21] Pearson: *Lifesaving, the story of the Royal Lifesaving Society* 1991.

1864, William Woodbridge, the swimming master of London's Victoria Park, produced *The Swimmers Practical Manual of Plain Facts and Useful Hints*. In it he writes about a Dr Bedale who was often seen floating on the river Mersey with a mast and sail secured to his body by a belt. Was he perhaps the first windsurfer of all time?

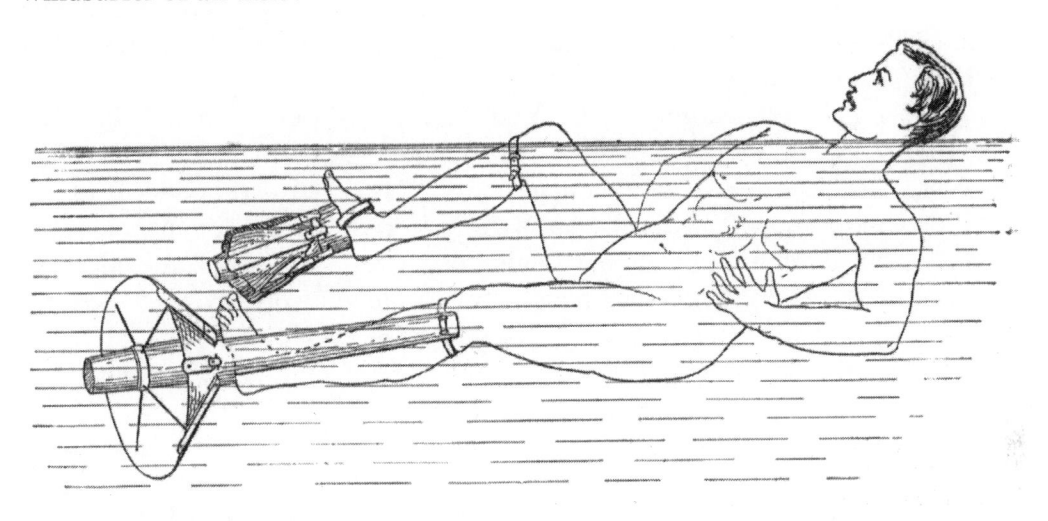

No swimmer should be without his 'Speedos'!

The Amateur Swimming Association (ASA) was founded in 1869 and a large number of clubs became affiliated with it, especially in the south of the country. Its objectives were to promote the art of swimming amongst both sexes and to encourage the teaching of swimming in schools. The ASA promoted water polo and endeavoured to improve public opinion in favour of swimming. Additionally it drew up consistent laws for organising competitions.

The French Connection

A milestone in British swimming history saw the successful cross channel swim by Captain Matthew Webb in 1875. As the crow flies, the distance from Dover to Calais is just less than eighteen miles, but tides and winds mean a longer distance has to be covered by the swimmer. It took Webb twenty-one hours forty-five minutes to complete the crossing. He then held on to the accolade of channel supremacy until 1911, when T W Burgess managed to swim across on his sixteenth attempt.

The effect of Webb's success had a dramatic impact on the nation's youth as reported in the *New York Times*:

Hung Out to Dry

> *'The London baths are crowded; each village pond and running stream contains youthful worshippers at the shrine of Webb and even along the banks of the river, regardless of the terrors of the Thames police, swarms of naked urchins ply their limbs, each probably determined that he one day will be another Captain Webb.'*

The 1880s saw a surge in swimming interest; there were now hundreds of swimming clubs with many members.

The first lady to swim the Channel was an American: Gertrude Ederle.[22] She took the world by storm, crossing in a record time of fourteen hours thirty-nine minutes. This remarkable woman not only knocked two hours off the record, but she also shifted the emphasis away from the male domination of the sport so evident up until then, encouraging many women to get involved in this form of healthful exercise. Swimmers between the ages of eleven and seventy years have since made many successful crossings.[23]

The interest of the public in swimming seemed insatiable. At the Music Hall, entertainment often centred on underwater acts. A glass tank would take centre stage and performers (scantily clad ladies being most popular), would stay under water for extended periods. They would drink from a bottle, undress, write on a slate, eat grapes and even smoke underwater. These novelties were the prelude to the main attraction: staying submerged for times approaching five minutes! The show would end in drama, as the performer would try to rise to the surface, but fail and have to be rescued. How much of this was part of the act it's hard to say, but it kept audiences on the edge of their seats and was the main draw.

Distance swimming also caught the imagination of many. One of the most popular events - the fifteen mile swim through London, first held in 1907 - was won by Mr J A Jarvis of Leicester. Lake Windermere hosted a sixteen-mile event, and all over the country similar proceedings drew big crowds.

Snatched from Death

The Royal Humane Society founded in 1774 had a receiving house built on land that King George III had donated, next to the Serpentine Lake in Hyde Park. It was considered at the time unlucky to rescue a drowning person and even more so, to attempt to resuscitate someone. Permission from the Mayor

---

[22] 1926.

[23] The youngest, Thomas Gregory (UK) - in 1988 at 11 years 330 days, the oldest, Roger Allsopp (UK) - in 2011 at 70 years and four months.

had to be obtained before a corpse could be landed, and the very idea of attempting to resuscitate an individual was seen as being on par with endeavouring to raise the dead. Such attempts were held even by men of eminence to be *'idle and visionary.'* Because of the superstitions surrounding such deaths, people were reluctant to come to the assistance of others. For example, it was considered unlucky to get wet when lifting a corpse from the water. Fishermen would not lift a drowned person into their boat but would tow the body behind it instead. They would not allow a pier to be used to receive the body as this was seen as potentially detrimental to the fishing industry. These superstitions probably originated from our Germanic ancestors, who believed that all accidental drownings were meant as sacrifices for an ill-tempered river spirit. To save a person from their fate, or worse still to resuscitate a person who was apparently dead, was seen as a sure way to bring calamity upon oneself. It was even believed that the rescued party, having been snatched from his destiny, might seek out the rescuer and cause him capital injury! Even those who managed to save themselves were sometimes viewed as being one of the living dead and thus they were shunned.

Disconcertingly, the RHS had on hand a deadly looking recovery device. A long pole with four lethal looking spikes enabled them to hook people out of the water, or to drag them up from the bottom. Although staff were on hand around the clock to aid individuals who had drowned in the lake, their success in saving lives was hampered by their naive methods. The apparently drowned person was to be pulled from the lake by his hair or in the case of baldness by the arm and placed into a bath of hot water in the receiving house. Thus, the warming of the individual took first priority, to be followed by attempts at resuscitation with the aid of bellows.[24] It was not until 1887 that a standardised, medically sound procedure materialised. Meanwhile many unnecessary deaths were the result. 'The Public Bath and Wash Houses Act' was amended in 1878, giving powers to local authorities to erect swimming pools for the people. According to the record books this was a particularly bad year for deaths by drowning: in England, 3,659 people met their end in this way! In the main, swimmers were either men or boys as women were given very little opportunity or encouragement to swim, but this was far from satisfactory. The need for things to change became apparent following a terrible disaster on the Thames. The steamboat *Princess Alice* sank with nearly three hundred and fifty female passengers on board, only one of whom survived: she, the only swimmer. This was probably due to the lack of swimming opportunities then available to women and the virtual non-existence of instruction for females. As

---

[24] Up until at least 1855.

Hung Out to Dry

SERPENTINE CLUB—CHRISTMAS MORNING.

swimming baths were provided predominantly for men, women found themselves restricted to a small number of establishments; the river and the sea. However, when owners realised that a large number of females were prepared to use the baths, they introduced special sessions. The next thirty years would see vast improvements.[25] Moral concerns had separated the sexes and British prudery had raised objections to the sight of female flesh,[26] but these unnatural attitudes were costing lives. If women had been encouraged to swim sooner, the disaster on the Thames might well have turned out quite differently. Just two years earlier, men and boys were moved out of the small lake in Victoria Park,

---

[25] The *Princess Alice* sank after a disastrous collision with the coal ship *Bywell Castle*, at Galleon's Reach on the River Thames on a return trip from the seaside. Only 69 of the pleasure boats passengers survived including just one woman. Approximately six hundred and forty lives were lost in all; September 3rd 1878. The Thames, thick with sewage, robbed most of those plunged into it of both breath and life.

[26] Victorian Britons found the sight of ladies' ankles erotic and even piano legs had skirts fitted for the sake of decency.

London and into the purpose - built concrete lined pool (pictured in the introduction). The boating lake in which they had swam since 1845 was then turned over for use by female swimmers. This, it is believed, is the very first attempt to accommodate women anywhere in Britain, with the exception of plunge pools.

The Royal Humane Society, although unsure of its procedures in the early days, did *prevent* many from drowning. For instance, in the year up until October 1911, the number of bathers using the Serpentine Lake was 275,745. With such large numbers attending, the Society made sure that boatmen were always present on the water to rescue anyone in trouble. During that year *not one* person drowned and all because of the watchful care of the Society. When you consider that up to 6,000 council school children would be bathing in the lake at a time, the boatmen's job cannot have been easy. On hot sunny days it was common for as many as 1,200 ordinary Londoners to come and bathe. The boatmen had rescued 34 people that had got into difficulties by this point, but not one of them required attention at the receiving house. This, I'm sure you will agree, is wonderful testament to the adage: *'prevention is better than cure.'*

For every argument there was in favour of swimming, there was always a counter-argument to advise against it, as drowning is an ever-present possibility near water. In 1891 the Royal Life-Saving Society began its work in teaching rescuers how to release themselves from the grip of a drowning person, which can so easily lead to the death of both. With the excellent instruction provided in recovery to the bank and in resuscitation, many unnecessary deaths were prevented. For example, Police Constable Alfred Taylor of the Bath City Police Force used this invaluable information when he came to the aid of an eight-year-old boy on August 24th 1911, saving his life:

> *'When about twenty yards away I saw the body being lifted from the water, where it had been for nearly fifteen minutes. The body was perfectly purple, the arms rigid, no sign of life whatever…the lad's limbs were so rigid that the arm had to be held in position under the forehead. I then proceeded to restore breathing…as laid down in the book of instructions issued by the R.L.S.S. this I continued for thirty minutes before any sign of life was observed.'*[27]

This account reveals something quite remarkable about the human body; we each have extraordinary qualities of self-preservation. When a person drowns in very cold water, the body reacts by slowing down vital processes. This means that resuscitation can successfully be achieved even after an extended period

---

[27] *The Complete Swimmer*: Franc Sachs 1912.

without breathing. It may take several minutes or even, as in this case, half an hour or more for the person to revive sufficiently for them to breathe for themselves; yet despite the fact that their brain has been short of oxygen, those revived generally suffer little or no lasting brain damage. The three R's: Release, Rescue and Resuscitation as instructed by the Society, led to the saving of many lives, and because of its excellent work, the Society received royal recognition at the behest of King Edward VII

'Dob Dob Dob'[28]

Robert Baden Powell wrote his book: *Scouting for Boys* and launched his world famous scouting movement in 1908, in it he says:

> *'Every boy should learn to swim. I've known lots of fellows pick it up the first time they try, others take longer… All you have to do is at first to try to swim like a dog, as if crawling along in the water. Don't try all at once to swim with the breaststroke. When paddling along like a dog, get a friend to support you at first with his hand under your tummy… When in camp, bathing will be one of your joys and one of your duties - a joy because it is such fun, a duty because no Scout can consider himself a full-blown Scout until he is able to swim and to save life in the water. But there are dangers about bathing for which every sensible Scout will be prepared.'*

Scouts were encouraged to select one or two good swimmers to oversee their friends. They were to be ready, undressed and prepared to jump in at any moment to help a bather who got into difficulties. The idea of scouts looking after themselves and providing their own life saving protection is an initiative that was common to the swimming public in general. People would watch out for each other and thus the need for lifeguards was not so pronounced. Baden Powell engendered self-sufficiency and community responsibility. He encouraged his scouts aged between eleven and fifteen to make themselves of use in a variety of practical ways; such as in putting out fires, directing traffic near road ac-

Opposite: Little children of the well-to-do receive swimming instruction, suspended like 'Little Tiddlers' in the Thames. (Wallingford 1906).

---

[28] This was the greeting given by boys to the Scout Master at each meeting, a group promise to: 'Do our best!'

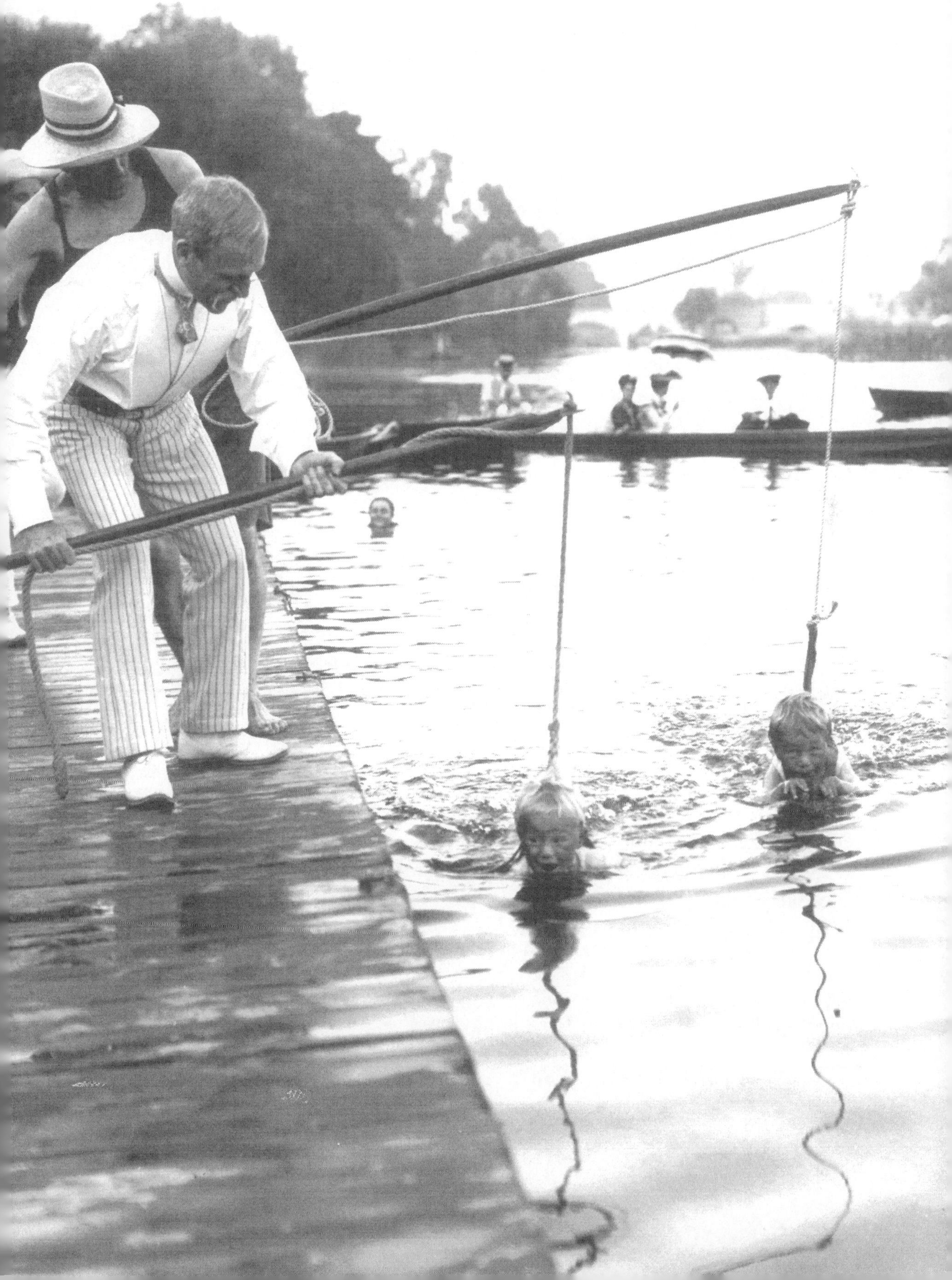

cidents, and in entering the water and saving the lives of people in difficulties. He did not just tell his boys to do this, but the scouting organisation taught the practical skills needed in order to do so safely. From 1910 the rescuer badge was awarded to those who could demonstrate their abilities.

Children were very much encouraged to become capable swimmers. The Board of Education had recommended that swimming be part of the curriculum since 1891, but it would be another twenty-seven years before the 'Education Act' empowered local authorities to establish school swimming baths in 1918.

Like a Duck to Water

With an improvement in safety records, the popularity of swimming increased even further. Take the Glasgow public swimming bath as an example. It attracted 602,864 bathers in the year ending May 1902 and each year the figure rose. By 1938, two million more bathers were using the baths annually. This means that for every person in Glasgow there were more than two swimming visits during the year. However there were always more males using the pool; they out numbered females three to one.

It can easily be seen that in the 20th Century swimming and bathing took on unbelievable popularity. Young men and boys in particular, were attracted to the baths due to the opportunities they offered; firstly for swimming instruction and then as their skills developed they came back repeatedly for the fun of the exercise. These pools were not of course free and so, despite the repeated chorus of the virtues of bathing, the majority of the public remained unresponsive. The social atmosphere at corporation venues was quashed by patronage and officialdom. Thus many could not bear to pay for the privilege of swimming when they could do it for free and without restrictions in their local lake or river. The experience of natural swimming bears no comparison with the stifled regimentation evident in many enclosed pools even today. Holidays by the sea were also popularising the movement away from the restrictions of authority, whilst the emancipation of women certainly brought about real liberation for female swimmers.

Just as in Roman times, swimming was once more seen as an essential skill. With the growth of the Empire, young men were to be trained as imperialists, with swimming being very much encouraged in public schools, such boys were the pride of the nation. Mr Hewitt of Marlborough was quoted as saying:

'Every boy here has to learn to swim unless he is forbidden to bathe by

the school doctor, or, of course, if, as has happened in very few cases, his parents do not wish him to bathe, or he can get them to say they do not wish it. I have only known this done in some half-dozen cases in my quarter of a century and it is an interesting, if tragic fact, that three of these boys have since been drowned.'[29]

Looking back at the swimming drills taught at public and corporation schools, the zeal with which authorities took up the challenge to reduce the risk of drowning can instantly be seen. The method began on *dry land* with the pupils standing with arms outstretched and learning to synchronise arm movements with their breathing, whilst at the same time practising the action of alternate legs. Following this, children took it in turns to lie prone on the back of their partner (at right angles), whilst being thus supported they practiced both arm and leg movements. Finally, the drill would continue in the water with the first pupil standing and operating his arms as he walked along in the pool shallows, his colleague would hold onto his shoulders and learn to synchronise his leg action to match the walker's arms. At a given signal he would let go of one shoulder and use the free arm to imitate his partner and at the next signal he would swim free and hopefully continue swimming. Forty or more pairs would be instructed at the same time and literally thousands soon gained their confidence.

Lifesaving was also taught and children of between twelve and fifteen years of age rapidly learnt to become capable lifesavers as shown by the following:

'Philip Mead aged twelve, a pupil at East Lane council school succeeded in saving George Rowden, aged fourteen, from drowning in the Thames on June 1st 1910. The boy Rowden was swimming at the foot of

---

[29] *The Complete Swimmer.* Frank Sacks: 1912.

Hung Out to Dry

East Lane stairs when he became exhausted and was carried out by the tide. The exhaustion was partly due to the strong tide and partly to his getting into the wash of a passing steamer. Philip Mead went to the lad's assistance and succeeded in bringing him to the side. The water where the rescue was effected was twelve feet deep and a water man states: "That but for Mead's timely aid, Rowden must have been drowned."'

Over in America, the Red Cross under the direction of Commodore Wilbert Longfellow launched their water safety program in 1914. Longfellow preferred to teach swimmers in the water rather than on dry land. This trend ultimately reached British shores, but success was not so quickly attained when teaching large numbers to swim. Even very young children were taught, suspended like tiddlers from a fishing rod. The freedom that swimming brought to the children mastering the skill was twofold. It meant, on the one hand, that boating and sea bathing privileges could be granted to them, and on the other, that the sparkling and inviting element was no longer a source of dread for child and parent alike.

Johnny Weissmuller: *Tarzan the Ape Man.*

Another influence came from Hollywood, in the *Tarzan* films starring Johnny Weissmuller. This Olympic champion became every boy's hero of the silver screen. They would act out the antics they had witnessed at the cinema, fighting with each other under water, imagining themselves as Tarzans struggling with crocodiles. Swimming was seen as both fun and manly, as was the distinctive Tarzan call. Other films such as *Footlight Parade* with its spectacular waterfall sequences went on to take swimming popularity to dizzy heights. Synchronized swimming displays and impressive diving exhibitions concreted the foundations of acceptability for future years, leading to the construction of yet more pools.

From Pride to Prejudice

The old model boat pond is taken over by children despite the cold! Teignmouth Devon, 1970.

Many lidos were opened, rising to a peak of popularity in the 1930s. Most sizeable towns now had a respectable establishment for swimming and this meant that those who could not swim began to feel behind the times. The majority of such lidos would include a series of diving boards, even though the water into which a diver plunged was often no more than six foot deep. By the end of the 20th Century, diving became unpopular due to the fear of accidents and the possibility of litigation. The Health and Safety Commission introduced strict safety standards late in the century, a move that led to the end of diving at most pools, resulting in a further reduction of swimming popularity especially among teenagers. Most of our open-air pools have since been closed due, in part to the availability of alternative forms of recreation. The television, internet and computer games captivate many and steal much of their leisure time. This, along with the advent of continental travel, which has introduced the general public to much warmer temperatures at swimming pools abroad, has meant a move away from the lido back home except on the sunniest of days. Although boys and young men remain the most intrepid group of swimmers today, the number of females that have taken up swimming has increased significantly in proportion with the steady increase in water temperature.

According to The Institute of Baths Management, 95% of users swim for fun in standing depth water,[30] of these, 85% are less than seventeen years of age and 50% are under twelve (well below wage earning age). Thus it can be seen that the largest group of swimmers have no voice at all when it comes to the regulation of swimming. Happily, there has been a move in recent years towards providing continental style fun pools, with slides and wave machines. These have in turn been met with eager enthusiasm on the part of the nation's youngsters and have succeeded in attracting great numbers. Butlin's Holidays were the first to capitalise on this need by investing huge sums of money in building extravagant 'water worlds' thus providing very warm bathing for their visitors. These complexes have formed the main attraction for this kind of holiday in recent years. As you might expect, they have proved especially popular to families with young children.

The Plug Is Pulled

Many moves were made to represent the rights of children in the 20th century but, sadly, swimming outdoors and, in some areas, even paddling pools have now become rare indeed. We may live at a time when children are seen to have many rights, but such rights are no substitute for the freedoms they have lost. River swimming, popular until the 1970s, is now discouraged almost everywhere. The reasons for this will surface in chapter five. Suffice to say here that something seems to change within us as we reach adulthood. The sheer exhilaration and joy that children experience in and around water somehow becomes frightening to their elders. Even those who enjoyed the experience themselves as children, grow up to view it as undesirable for today's youth.

River bathing nowadays is nowhere near as popular as it used to be. Swimming in the great outdoors is tolerated at best, but rarely is it encouraged except at the seaside. The key to these changes and the consequences that swimmers feel, will unfold as the story develops. But for now, we should note that the young people of today must find it hard to fully respect the authority of a society that is seen by them as directly restricting their freedom and enjoyment.

Many schemes have been launched in an endeavour to civilise the wayward youths that seem hell-bent on destroying the security of responsible

---

[30] Not more than 1.2 meters deep. Perrin: *Sports Halls and Swimming Pools* 1980.

citizens. It should, however, be remembered that free access to river and lake provide just the sort of outlet that such youngsters need and may well, for a time at least, discourage subversive activities that they might otherwise have engaged in.

A disproportionate number of the young males that ultimately find their way into young offenders' institutions are afflicted with the learning difficulty of dyslexia[31] (approaching 50%). In order to save money, the education system fails to fully recognise the needs of such youngsters (predominately boys), with the exception of Swansea LEA who have been working to address the problem since 1997. Education Authorities throughout the rest of the country still entertain a preference in many primary schools to wait until children fall behind in their education by three to four years before offering any specific assistance. By such time, many children have given up in their efforts at school, being convinced that they are either lazy or stupid. Teachers often express their disappointment with such children, as there is often a marked difference between a dyslexic child's achievement and his obvious intelligence (many teachers actually insist that such children are lazy, refusing to acknowledge any disability whatsoever). Academic failure leads to disruption in the classroom, feelings of low self worth and for some, to a life of crime. Although many dyslexics find sports challenging due to co-ordination difficulties, most excel in the swimming pool. It is not surprising then, to find that more than a few of these young boys bunking off from school are drawn to open water for recreation. Many are excluded from school because of their behavioural problems, only to suffer social exclusion at the riverside as members of the public frown on their activities. The build-up in feelings of isolation and resentment are a prelude to a life of poverty and violence in many cases. Regardless of the amount of money required to fight crime, it seems that the 'powers that be' would much sooner spend a thousand pounds a week on detention; as opposed to twenty pounds a week on special needs education.[32]

Money is always in short supply, but a lesson taught by our Roman forbears may be worth reiterating here. The proverb: *'An ignorant man neither*

---

[31] *Times Education Supplement;* 29-10-99 p 4-9.

[32] There are many exercise programs that improve a dyslexic's performance by, in effect, rewiring the sufferer's brain ('Brain Gym' for example). Sadly, the radical nature of this approach has been given the cold shoulder by the education establishment despite the fact that its success in other countries is well documented. A fairly new development is found in the work of Ruth Miskin. Her programme to teach new readers (as well as 11-12 year olds who have so far failed to gain any real mastery of reading) is having striking success. From ABC to Fluency is being achieved through careful teaching and a fully structured approach, despite the learning difficulties of dyslexia.

Hung Out to Dry

knows how to read nor to swim,' shows the importance placed on education by the Romans as their empire embraced the world. We would do well to learn from their example in setting priorities.

A puzzling anomaly exists in my home town of Leicester. The City Council has insufficient funds to provide pedestrian crossings and traffic calming schemes in all areas and so they concentrate on those with high accident or death rates. Inevitably, a number of people die or are injured each year as victims of the motorcar. On the other hand, money *is* available to deter swimmers from venturing into open waters, despite the lack of incidents connected with swimming. The reasons for this paradox take some unravelling, but it is interesting to note that swimmers are singled out for control. Victorian ideals with respect to keeping the general public under firm rule are very evident in the life of the swimmer.

A hot summer holiday by the river, lake or sea gives rise to rich happy memories that can last a lifetime. Caution is needed of course, as drowning is a real possibility. But for those who have tasted the forbidden fruits of open water swimming, the loss of liberty when authorities try to stifle it are keenly felt. British pride in its swimming empire has now given way to prejudice. The lack of competition pools, diving facilities and encouragement is symptomatic of our changed perception of swimming. We may have led the world into the water, but now the world is beating us at our own game. Why is it that unlike the rest of Europe, in Britain we are so keen to control those who wish to swim in natural inland settings? Why have swimmers fallen from grace? To understand our distinctive attitude towards swimmers, we first need to understand the development of our unique culture, and the influence swimmers have had upon its growth. Here in Britain we have turned our back on our swimming tradition. Many diverse factors have come into play, turning the pride we so keenly felt early in the 20th century into the prejudice so evident today.

The information we have considered so far sketches the rough outline of swimming history in Britain. But there is more to this history than meets the eye. Having considered the facts, we will now dip beneath the surface and look at the reasons behind the swimmer's demise. In time we will look at the seaside holiday and the popularity of sunbathing, but first we will consider the reasons behind Christendom's war on swimming and bathing, as we examine two perceived opposites: cleanliness and godliness.

Opposite: The wooden diving tower erected at Henleaze Lake Bristol in the 1920s (See chapter 7). The photograph was taken in 1932.

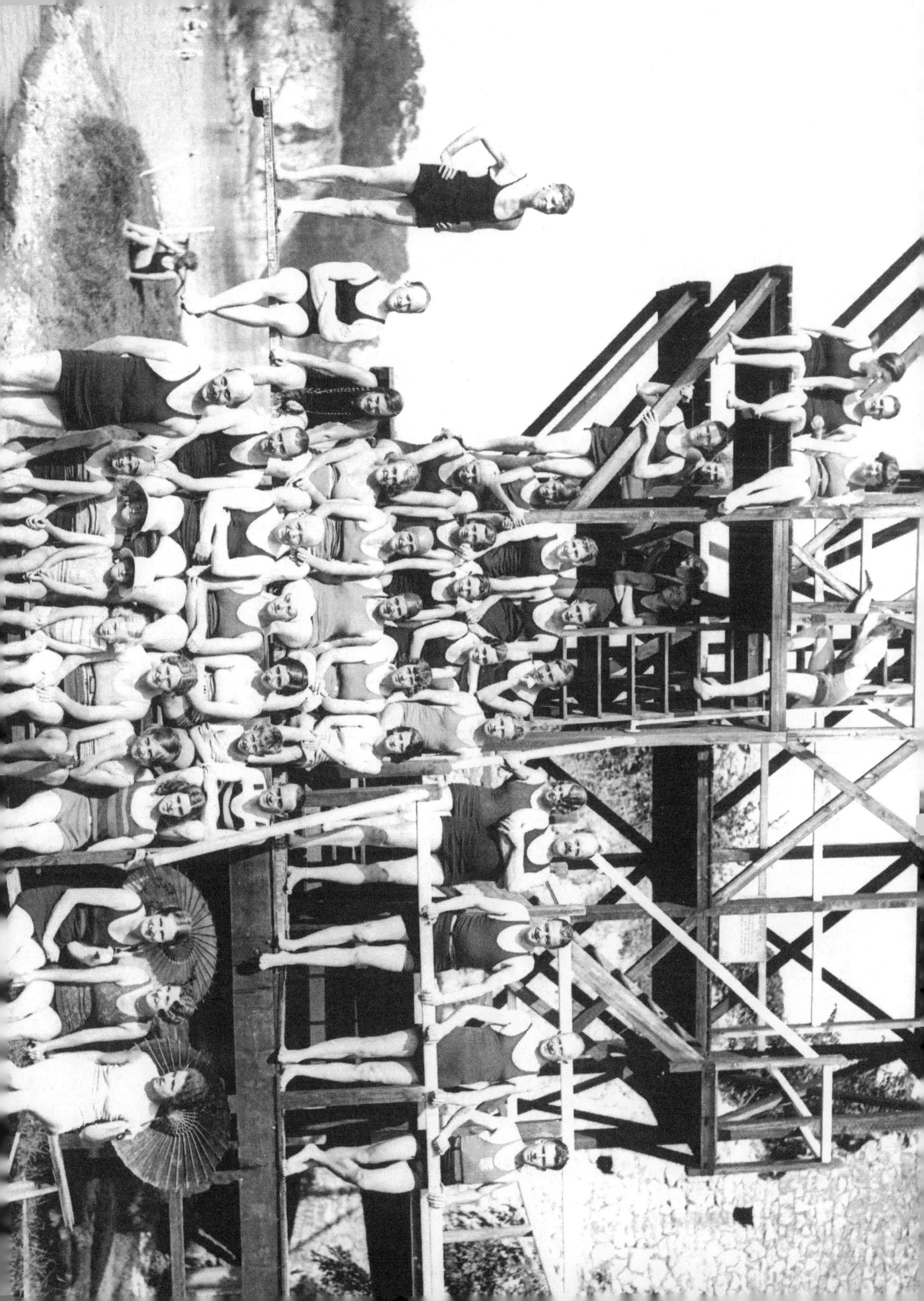

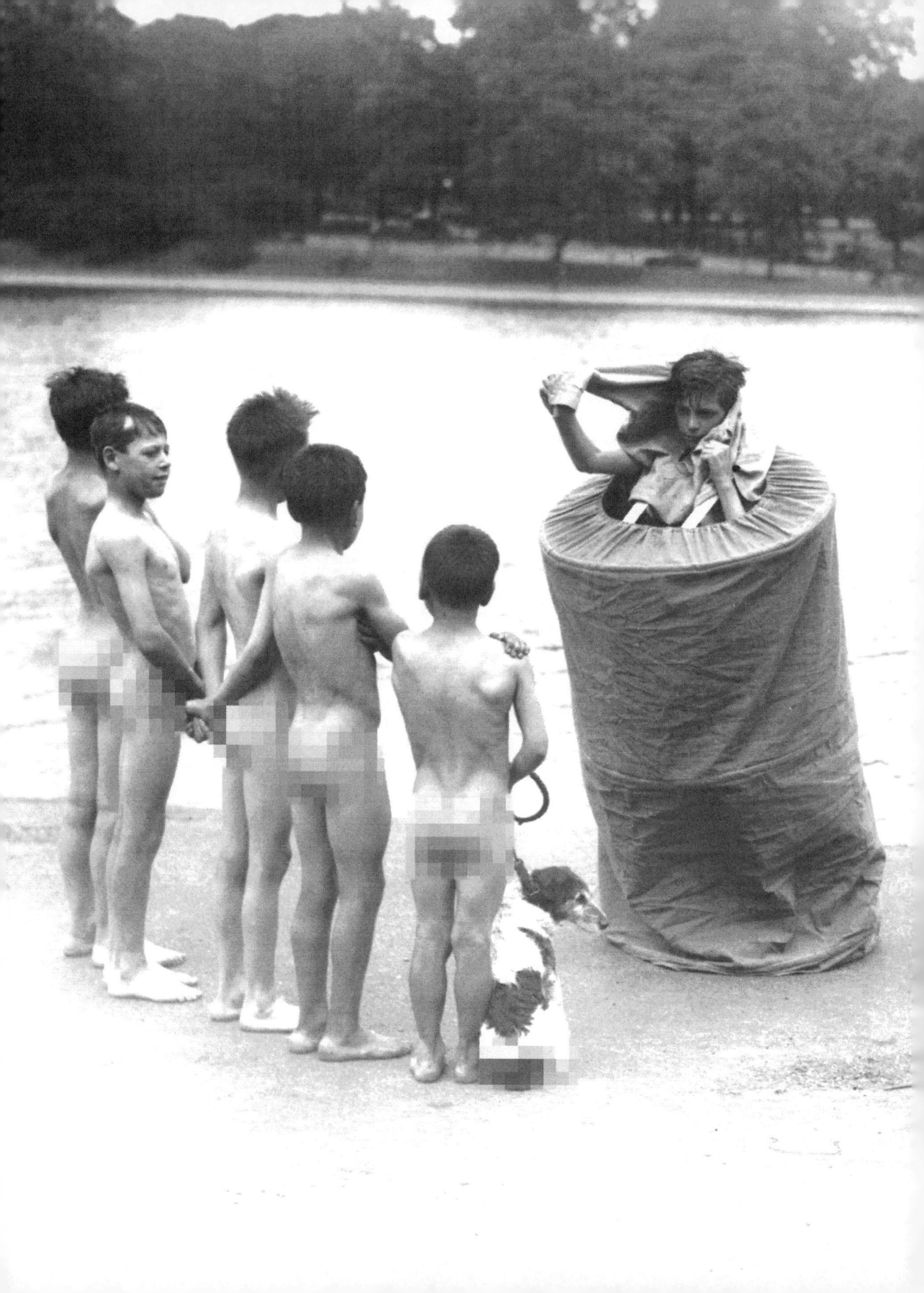

Chapter 2
Cleanliness versus Godliness

We cannot possibly discuss the history of swimming without mentioning the influence of religion. Many will quite naturally assume religion to be completely divorced from our subject and for this they are forgiven, as its influence has rarely been discussed. However, when you have considered this chapter, I am confident you will hold a different view. You will see that Christendom's leaders, albeit with the best of motives, have dealt swimming and bathing a cruel blow during their period of control. By misapplying Bible texts and by making assumptions regarding the thinking of God, much harm was done during the Christian era, especially to women and children.

The Good Book

The Bible is arguably the most influential religious book in the world. Certainly it is the most widely distributed and translated work known to man. What then does the Bible actually say about swimming? An early reference to it uses a swimmer to illustrate the downfall of an enemy nation - Moab.[33] There are varying interpretations as to the meaning of this verse. Some see Moab as a swimmer who forlornly tries to preserve his life in a hopeless situation (with the nation pictured as a drowning man). This interpretation sees swimming in an unfavourable light. On the other hand, God could be seen as the one that slaps out his hands like a swimmer to devastate Moab. If God is pictured as the swimmer, a view that sits well with the context of the verse, the activity can hardly be condemned. Despite this, the Christian apologist Jerome of the 4th Century took the negative view, comparing the fate of the swimmer with that of

Opposite: Working class boys were the last to be convinced of the need to be ashamed of nakedness. This photograph taken in Hyde Park, July 1939, shows working class interest in the middle class obsession with 'decency' as an older boy uses a Skreenette at the lido.

---

[33] Isaiah 25:11 (778 BCE) the Moabites were descendants of Lot, the nephew of Abraham. Having left the service of God, they chose other gods for themselves developing a hard-set enmity towards Israel.

the damned. Needless to say, swimming was not encouraged during his reign of influence. Perhaps his preconceptions regarding God's view of bathing coloured his judgment. Today we may well see cleanliness as next to godliness, but such was not the case in the time of Jerome. The context of the verse may indicate that God is the one pictured as the swimmer, but this view would have gone contrary to what was 'known' at the time; in fact, it might well have been viewed as heresy. On this one verse hung the fate of the swimmer for centuries. The Bible was not against swimming, but religious leaders taught otherwise. By misapplying the text to make it fit in with Church doctrine, God's views regarding cleanliness were brushed aside in favour of a Church morality that was neither practical nor healthy.

On the other hand the book of Ezekiel describes a stream deep enough to swim in. [34] If this were the only other mention of swimming in the Scriptures it would still be seen as a skill familiar to man and, more importantly, acceptable to God. Yet the Bible has more to say. In the Christian era, the apostle Peter is described as plunging into the sea and presumably swimming to Jesus on the seashore.[35] And finally, we have the Apostle Paul's experience when shipwrecked near Malta, and the advice given to swimmers as well as non-swimmers regarding their survival.[36] It's obvious then that swimming was recognised as a skill with life-preserving benefits, here approved by one of the founders of the early Church. Had Jerome rather than Jesus witnessed Peter's plunge into the sea, would he have been damned rather than blessed?

With regard to bathing, the Bible repeatedly refers to the need to keep clean and to bathe all of one's flesh to maintain cleanliness. In addition, it sets high standards of morality without resorting to prudishness in covering sexuality. The Law of Moses, for instance, includes direction on the disposal of human waste,[37] adherence to which ensured the purity of both the drinking water and the bathing waters of the Israelites.

Carnal Thoughts

With the death of the apostles, Christianity changed beyond recognition in its beliefs and attitudes. The Bible was no longer perceived as the only source of divine guidance, and in the 4th century Jerome expounded the view that sex was sinful. He felt that, even in marriage, sex was wrong and that virgins were the

---

[34] Ezekiel 47:5 (591 BCE).
[35] John 21:7.
[36] Acts 27:42-44.
[37] Deuteronomy 23:12-13.

Cleanliness versus Godliness

only individuals retaining God's full approval. Strange as it may now seem, at this time filth and morality were seen to hold hands. Jerome lavished praise on nuns who would never let water touch their bodies, especially those who were crawling with lice.[38] Augustine of Hippo was to follow in his footsteps. Despite the lustful excesses of his youth, he converted to Christianity and navigated the Church away from godly thinking on matters of sex. His crusade against intimacy evidenced a newfound loathing for carnal knowledge. He reinterpreted the Bible's account of the original sin, transforming it into a crime of sexual passion. Until this point in time, the eating of the forbidden fruit detailed in Genesis had been seen by the Church as an act of disobedience, but Augustine re-invented it as a crime of sexual temptation. By his thinking, lust had caused the expulsion from Eden. Eve had tempted Adam into sexual acts, thus condemning them both.[39] Overlooked, however, is the reality that God had expressly commanded the first human pair to have children.[40] Sexual relations then, in obedience to God's command for this first married couple would hardly bring God's condemnation. Rather, it was Augustine's moral conflicts during childhood and his later obsession with sex which led to the disapproval of his mother, a devout Catholic. These events, not those occurring in the Garden of Eden, led him to rename the genitals as pudenda, meaning parts to be ashamed of, and therefore to sex becoming synonymous with sin. The sight of the naked body became shameful even for private bathing and especially so once the offending parts began to develop at puberty.

Even prior to this, the Roman association with bathing was seen by the Church as immoral. The Roman baths had become a magnet for prostitutes, pimps and procurers. All kinds of sexual vice prevailed, and because the Christian movement had by now gained political power, its leaders waged war upon bathing. They argued that the only way they could eliminate the evils bathing had brought was to wage war upon bathing itself, even if such a war meant its extermination lock, stock and barrel. The Roman lifestyle of pleasure-seeking was totally divergent to the Christian way, as evidenced by the debauchery so rife at the baths. Many of these baths included private cubicles and this privacy, combined with mixed bathing, led to the arrival of a large number of illegitimate children. Because of such misconduct, mixed bathing was ultimately condemned.

---

[38] Bertrand Russell: *History of Western Philosophy*: 'cleanliness was viewed with abhorrence. Lice were called 'pearls of God,' and were a mark of saintliness. Saints male and female would boast that water had never touched their feet except when they had to cross rivers.'
[39] Simon Andreae: *Anatomy of Desire*.
[40] Genesis 1:27-28.

Bad Habits

Things were getting out of hand; nuns were taking off their habits when visiting the spas of Europe, and young girls requested in their marriage contracts the privilege to visit the spas without their husbands. But this desire to bathe in hot water led to conflict with the Church, and thus the expression *'getting into hot water'* was coined regarding persons that were heading for trouble. The condemnation of the Church meant that all over Europe the comfortable Roman baths fell into disuse and ruin. Bathing in the hot springs of Europe was considered as fit only for those worshipping the Devil. Those resisting Church teachings were condemned as degenerates. If bathing had to be practised at all, it would only be tolerated if such took place using cold water as a precaution to protect the bather's morality.

Of course, a very important exception to the 'no bathing rule' related to baptism. When one came to be baptised, water was seen as both a cleansing and purifying agent that passed on its benefits to the participant. Total immersion was seen as essential for salvation,[41] irrespective of the time of year, the age, or the circumstances of the individual. Constantine postponed his baptism until his death was approaching. At the age of 65 he offered himself for baptism in his 'birthday suit' in order to gain forgiveness for a lifetime of sins. His state of undress was not unusual, as it was the practice of the Church for all candidates to be baptised in the nude. Needless to say however, men and women were baptised in either separate parts of a river, in different enclosures, or failing this at different times of the day.[42] As the Church developed, it was decided that even infants should be baptised, despite the fact that this contradicted Jesus's instruction wherein only disciples or taught ones were to be immersed.[43] Augustine of Hippo modified Jesus's command, teaching that baptism cleansed an infant from original sin. Any infant that passed away prior to baptism was thereafter to be consigned to the 'fires of hell'. During his ministry however, Jesus expressed a very different view, welcoming un-baptised infants and praising their meekness.[44]

The Church propounded the belief that once a Christian was baptised, he gained purification and would remain spiritually and physically clean for the rest of his life. Henceforth there would be no further need for washing or bathing. This precaution against bathing was seen as protecting Christians from sinful thoughts directed towards themselves or others, and from the damnation that

---

[41] Following the example of Christ. Baptism - Greek ba′pti·sma, literally means immersion.
[42] Scott: *The Story of Baths and Bathing* 1939.
[43] Matthew 28:19-20.
[44] Luke 18:15-17, Jeremiah 7:31.

would surely result. Water was considered to be a holy cleanser and there were many superstitions surrounding its allegedly magical properties. It was felt that water in its purity, would accept only individuals that were free from guilt, repelling the unworthy. Thus, a person's being accepted by water at baptism was seen as proof of his holiness. It was also held that baptismal waters would refuse to accept a guilty individual. This reasoning led to the ducking or 'the cold water ordeal' as it was known, which was commonly used until the 13th century as a means of determining the guilt or innocence of persons whose character was in doubt. It's not surprising then, that people developed an illogical and superstitious fear of water. The teaching that water would eject such ungodly souls was obviously flawed. Yet the Roman baths had developed into a hotbed of immorality; sinners were witnessed as floating upon the waters just like their father the Devil. Despite the fact that this teaching could be found nowhere in the Bible, it was adopted, and zealously applied for centuries; bad news for would-be swimmers!

The Swimming of Witches

It was asserted by many ecclesiastics and scientists that witches and wizards, through their communion with the Devil, became like him, lighter than air and would therefore not sink if thrown into water.[45] In the light of this knowledge, we can well imagine the scene as a child falls into a river and disappears beneath the surface. Anguish and grief on the part of the parents might well turn into despair should the child struggle to remain afloat, for such would be evidence of her previously undetected association with witchcraft! King James I's ruling in the early 17th century recommended that the 'ordeal' (the swimming of witches) should continue to be used in certain circumstances, on the grounds that water would reject witches, because such creatures had *'shaken off the sacred water of baptism'* So we can see that even at this late date, swimming was still seen by many as an unwholesome exercise.[46]

The skill of swimming, or even remaining afloat in the rivers of England at some periods in history was certainly nothing to be proud of. If you bathed

---

[45] Suffolk produced a high proportion of witches in comparison to the rest of the country. Locally grown rye grass became diseased, infected by the fungus ergot (*Claviceps Purpurea*). When made into bread and ingested in sufficient quantity it caused ergotism, resulting in hallucinations similar to those induced by LSD, along with many other physical effects including tremors and a sensation of prickling as though ants were crawling on the skin. It was assumed that sufferers had been bewitched and many innocent women were condemned as a result of ignorance regarding the true cause.

[46] *Daemonologie* 1597 (the last woman was burned to death as a witch in 1722).

you were seen as a degenerate, with filthy morals, and if you swam you became like the Devil himself! For many years, paintings that depicted the baby Jesus enjoying his first bath were quite popular. In the mid 1500s however, a meeting of priests resulted in such pictures being banned. The reasoning being that Jesus was perceived as so pure that bathing would be quite unnecessary. These ideas lasted a long time. Prior to the First World War, very little accommodation was made in London's hotels for bathing; in fact Park Lane was the first hotel to provide a bathroom for every bedchamber[47] In the USA, the White House had its first bathroom installed in 1851. It seems then that the adage: *'cleanliness is next to godliness'* was far from the minds of those directing the faith of Christians here in England and elsewhere throughout most of its history.[48]

The cloudy waters of time restrict our view of the past, but it would seem that in the 12th Century, bathing started to make a comeback. The Church's condemnation of hedonism was modified, as the virtues of bathing were extolled by physicians. However, the carryover was that bathing remained for health purposes only and many rules and regulations prevented participants bathing just for pleasure.

Dirty Waters

Ironically, healthful bathing was virtually impossible at this time, due to the uncleanliness of the water and the pollutants deposited in it. The bodies of the many patrons using the bathhouses were in a filthy state. So, in 1350 when bubonic plague[49] reached its peak, many of the baths were closed and those that did not, were in reality little more than brothels. From the 13th to the 15th centuries it was customary for girls to serve knights in the bath. *'The sexes bathed together and not innocently.'*[50] Banwell wrote in 1449: *'...a report has reached the bishop that the heavenly gift of the warm healing waters with which the City of Bath has been endowed from of old is turned into an abuse by the shamelessness of the people of that city...'*. Bath was notorious for the practice of mixed bathing and in 1450 Bishop Beckyngton threatened to excommunicate anyone entering the baths in a state of nakedness. Sexual vice became rampant and the baths were in a filthy state. Ecclesiastical authorities could do little. Al-

---

[47] *News of the World*: July 17th 1938.
[48] During the 18th and 19th Centuries, the unhygienic conditions in Europe and the United States caused missionaries to begin preaching a 'doctrine of cleanliness.' Filth was equated with sin, whereas cleanliness brought one closer to God. The Salvation Army went onto preach: 'Soap, Soup and Salvation.'
[49] Also known as the Black Death; it ultimately killed nearly half the population of Europe.
[50] Summer W. 1907. Folkways: A study of Mores, Manners, Customs and Morals

Cleanliness versus Godliness

though they condemned bathing as sinful and in some cases forbade the clergy from entering such establishments, their counsel fell upon deaf ears, and condemnations continued in vain. John Wood the elder writes: *'The Baths were like so many beer gardens and modesty was entirely shut out of them; people of both sexes bathing by day and night naked.'* Crowds came to watch the spectacle, but this did little to quell the desire of the aristocracy to attend. Although the bath was seen as a cure for all manner of diseases, the immorality of those benefiting from the cure led to the spread of venereal disease. The dread of VD meant that over a period of time the baths were left (for the most part) to prostitutes and their clients. Bath came to be known as the *'premier resort of frivolity and fashion.'* Things were much the same in France: thus in 1546 all such stew houses were demolished. Here in Britain, Henry VIII banned mixed bathing on moral grounds

The reformation had brought changes to the minds of those that held water to have magical powers. The Holy Wells scattered about the country lost their holiness, and became wishing wells instead. The doctor's scientific recommendations replaced superstition, again drawing crowds to the bath. Along with this popularity, moral concerns resurfaced. Bathing had proved to be too much fun to continue merely as a form of medication and so it soon regained acceptance as a pleasurable past time. As the rich wallowed in the luxury of the hot bath, along came the indiscretions of prostitutes, once more detracting from the nobility of the waters.

In the 16th century it was suggested that the wider use of undershirts, vests and pants, meant that for the clean-minded, bathing could be abandoned. Garments could be changed and washed, so there was absolutely no need to risk morality by washing the flesh. The bath again came to be looked upon as approved only by the depraved and immoral, and it would be another hundred years before bathing would return to respectable popularity. Even when it did, these attitudes simmered away under the surface as we saw in the extract from the *Gentleman's Magazine* on page 20.

By 1663 Sir Alexander Fraser was recommending that King Charles II should drink from the City of Bath's waters. His doing so again added to Bath's popularity and soon lodging houses nearby were charging as much as one guinea a night to stay in the town. It was later realised that drinking the water in which persons suffering from all manner of diseases had bathed themselves was surely unhealthy. *'So while little Tabby was washing her rump, the ladies kept drinking out of a pump.'* Not a pleasant prospect! Thus, opinion was changing on the healthful nature of such treatments.

Moral concerns persisted so that finally the ecclesiastical authorities won the day with ladies and gentlemen being admitted on alternate days. On the down side, the success of this order against mixed bathing resulted in a marked decrease in the number of those attending the bath. Even so, the link between immorality and bathing continued. In 17th century London, the sweating baths were notorious as havens for male and female homosexuals. The rubbers and attendants were seen as nothing more than perverts. Many were professional catamites, willing to work in the establishment without wages purely because of the opportunities working there presented.

The Christian faith faced a real dilemma. On the one hand it wanted to promote a lifestyle devoid of pleasure and especially sexual pleasure, whilst at the same time the benefits of bathing could not be denied. Yet how could they allow the general population, and especially common people, the privilege of bathing, when they were perceived as being immoral in the extreme?

Over in Japan, a bathing culture had developed which proved very appealing, especially to the working classes. A Japanese proverb: *'bathing buddies are the best of friends'* illustrates the attraction. They also had concerns over segregation, not of the sexes, as was our experience, but rather of the classes, as they were keen to maintain their social structure. Despite mixed nudity, the history of the Japanese bath lacks the scandal of the Roman and British experience. Daily, families bathed together with their children, and they felt no shame in their nakedness.[51] Here in Britain, the people had been so restrained by religious oppression and feelings of guilt that once clothing was removed for bathing,[52] the sensation of freedom and nudity led them to lose all self-control. The working classes were seen as devoid of all morals and restraint, and so they needed to be taken in hand for the sake of their health and salvation. The upper classes were seen as little better, they would indulge their every whim without thought to propriety. This left the middle classes to restore balance and control, and this they did through their professional positions and political offices. Thus the middle classes took responsibility for the shaping of British culture.

A Cruel Cut

Over in America, the 1860s saw circumcision introduced to control *childhood* sexuality. John Harvey Kellogg (Seventh Day Adventist) was a leading promoter of circumcision along with his other health cure – Kellogg's Cornflakes, which, it was said, could free a person from the urge to masturbate. In his book

---

[51] Japan is blessed with some 2,839 hot springs.
[52] 'Christians' were taught that it was shameful to look at even their own naked bodies so as to avoid temptation. Nakedness became synonymous with sin.

of 1888: *Plain facts for old and young*, he states: *'A remedy for masturbation which is almost always successful in small boys is circumcision. The operation should be performed by a surgeon **without administering an anaesthetic**, as the brief pain attending the operation will have a salutary effect upon the mind, especially if it is connected with the idea of punishment, as it may well be in some cases.'*

Patients in hospitals for the insane were observed to be habitual masturbators and it was assumed that this vice was the cause of their insanity. It was then believed that semen was manufactured by harvesting resources from the blood stream and that masturbation depleted essential reserves, debilitating those who abused themselves to the point that they would become physically and mentally enfeebled.[53] Clerics felt no need to rely on the Bible for guidance on the matter (see footnote 55). Despite the fact that the Law of Moses omits to cite the practice and that it is not specifically mentioned elsewhere in scripture, they felt sure that it was an unnatural act (it could never be procreative), and therefore it was judged to be a mortal sin, greater in gravity than fornication or adultery. As the guilty supposedly faced eternal damnation in a fiery hell, it was felt essential, especially for children, to be protected from such a fate at all costs. Childhood mortality was then much more common, thus a sense of urgency impelled many parents to welcome the circumcision of their children as a route to salvation. Although unable to stamp out the practice of self abuse entirely, by removing much of the organ during surgery they sought to reduce the frequency of indulgence by decreasing the pleasure obtained.[54]

Reinforcing such attitudes, in 1891 the English surgeon Jonathon Hutchinson advised the operation as a measure to prevent disease and disorders, but his premise remained the same. He writes:

> *'Measures more radical than circumcision would if public opinion permitted their adoption be a true kindness to many patients of both sexes.'*

Regarding one unfortunate he continues:

> *'Clarence was addicted to the secret vice practised among boys. I performed circumcision. He needed the rightful punishment of cutting pains after his illicit pleasures.'*

---

[53] The tract *Onania* was published in 18th Century England by clergyman Dr Bekkers as a warning to all. Masturbation was implicated as the prime cause of disorders in the body; it was even suggested that it could lead to death.

[54] In some cases, as much as 80% of the highly sensitive skin was removed, exposing the internal structures which themselves desensitise with time, contributing to impotence in later years.

Hung Out to Dry

This change of tack would have dire consequences for many children. When masturbation was considered merely as a sin, true repentance would lead to salvation.[55] However, once it was perceived that a child's health might be involved, people became much more worried. Ideas that circumcision helped prevent all manner of diseases gained quick acceptance in both America and the UK, especially among the upper middle classes.[56] Hysterical claims were made promoting this outrageous practice; hailed as a cure for anything and everything, which was really a cover up for the abuse that medics had inflicted on countless terrified boys.[57] When problems surfaced, they could not bring themselves to admit that they had made a terrible mistake. Great stress was now being placed on cleanliness and the operation came to be seen as an essential modification to the human male. Many felt confident, thinking that because God introduced circumcision in Bible times there could surely be no harm in it. This was a view that our European partners remained unconvinced about, and their reluctance to 'jump on the bandwagon' meant that the sexual mutilation of boys was thankfully limited to the Anglo-American union, along with those countries over whom it held sway. In Britain today, we still circumcise more than 22,000 boys each year,[58] 12,200 in hospitals (mostly babies), along with thousands more in private clinics and in the community, figures grossly out of proportion to numbers in the rest of Europe. In America roughly 80% are circumcised, compared to about 2% in Sweden.

Circumcision, as practised by Abraham and his descendants, was an operation that removed only a small amount of skin. The change to today's drastic type of surgery is the result of a knee jerk reaction to the evangelical success of the early Christians. During the 1st century, Jewish religious leaders were horrified to see thousands of Jews deserting their faith to become Christians. What made things worse was that these Christians would not circumcise their infants. Added to this, some of Jewish descent were having their condition reversed, in order to compete in the Greek Games[59] (competitors ran naked and Greek cul-

---

[55] The advent of the sexual revolution sees children today all but encouraged to experiment with masturbation. Young children question their sexual orientation and internet pornography educates them about sex. Without moral guidance they embark on a lifestyle that desensitises their conscience, erodes family values and dismantles the security of society.

[56] They wished to distance themselves from the debauched aristocracy just as much as from the perverse working classes.

[57] There was never any truth in the claims that amputation of the foreskin improved a boy's chances of better health.

[58] According to the Department of Health (*The Times* April 5th 2004).

[59] 1 Corinthians 7:18-19 expresses the thought that circumcision means 'nothing', yet by 140 CE this minor biblical procedure, approved by Moses and Abraham, changed radically to what is now known as circumcision today; see footnote 60.

ture objected to the rude appearance of the circumcised male). Thus, the Jewish identity came under threat, and this was a situation that could not be allowed to continue. Consequently the Jews determined to change the circumcision procedure in order to remove as much skin as possible, ensuring that once marked as Jewish, devotees would permanently remain so.[60] The resultant operation was not only much more painful and dangerous, but it also caused considerable damage to the organ.[61] It has since been found that amputation of the foreskin has many damaging side effects both physical and psychological.[62] In some cases it has tragically led to the death of the infant or child. Babies feel pain more acutely than older children and adults. Despite the evident distress of infants, the procedure is still being performed without anaesthetic,[63] the resultant trauma being another cause for concern.[64] Needless to say, cultures that promote the new mutilating circumcision resist any suggestion that harm could result, mainly because to do so would mean admitting that the promoters (who are usually themselves mutilated), had been damaged and denial is a protective response. Additionally, because of circumcision's biblical origin, modern Christians see any criticism of it, as a criticism of Almighty God, not realising that modern day circumcisions are nothing like those described in the Scriptures.

Concerns regarding sexuality became paramount. Baden Powell, founder of the Boy Scout movement, advised Scouts on the dangers of masturbation, recommending a cold bath to help reduce improper thoughts. Research into the effects of bathing in cold-water reveals that in fact it has the opposite effect,

---

[60] Three Hebrew words are used to describe different forms of circumcision. Milah, or biblical circumcision, was practiced up until 140 CE and involved the removal of only the tip of the foreskin as depicted in Michelangelo's statue of *David*. Periah, became universal by about 140 CE. The tissue of the glans and foreskin are usually joined at birth, often not separating naturally until mid-childhood or even late into adolescence. Periah tears the tissue apart and sees most of the shaft skin cut away laying the glans bare and making the mutilation irreversible. Messisa: practiced from around 500-625 CE is the same as Periah, but the Mohel goes on to suck on the mutilated organ with his mouth in order to draw blood and then he spits wine onto the wound.

[61] From its inception the Jews were commanded to circumcise their infants on the eighth day even if this conflicted with the Sabbath. Despite the fact that the original operation was minor in nature, blood clotting factors such as Vitamin K and prothrombin reach a lifetime peak on this day thus protecting the child from excessive bleeding.

[62] Circumcised boys are often ashamed of their unnatural appearance whilst being simultaneously curious regarding the physiology of normal boys. This combination can lead them into difficulties. Various charities have been set up around the world such as NORM-UK, to provide medical expertise regarding alternatives to circumcision for adults and children.

[63] In America and in the UK when amputations are performed in the community.

[64] Goldman: *Circumcision the Hidden Trauma*.

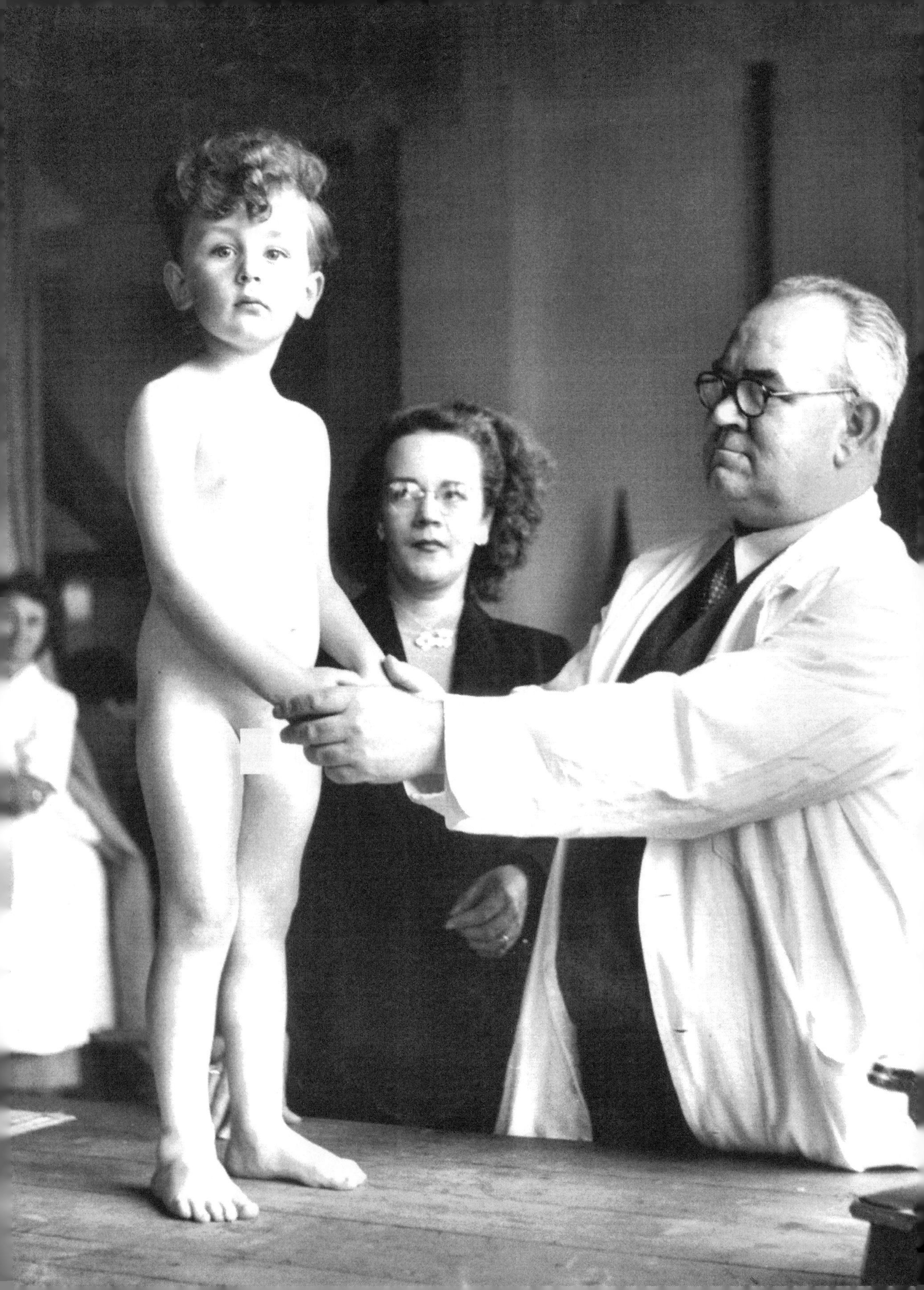

Opposite: Doctor knows best? This image featured in an article questioning the wisdom of baby competitions: Picture Post (1952).

raising the level of testosterone and with it sexual desire. On the positive side though, his advice would have helped raise levels of immunity, lower body fat and increase the bather's sense of well-being due to the body's reaction to cold water. Even so, boys were monitored during the night whilst on camping trips to ensure that they slept on their sides rather than on their backs or stomachs, as it was felt that this could lead them into pleasuring themselves and to dire consequences in the afterlife. Boys were awakened and repositioned if found sleeping in a way that might lead into temptation. Such 'protection' was not seen as in any way intrusive; rather it was viewed as evidence of paternal care and concern for the everlasting well being of God-fearing youths.

The prevailing view of the Church throughout this period was that the British public had very low morals and were in need of protection and guidance if they were to avoid the danger of eternal damnation. Britons had been flocking to the coast to experience the pleasure and benefits of sea bathing. Swimming itself was rising to a popularity that could well be compared to that of football today, but men and boys had been swimming naked, which worried the middle classes. Fears over the moral implications that might result from the enjoyment of such experiences; the popularity of nude bathing and of the sexes bathing together culminated in a middle class effort to control working class behaviour, with a comprehensive list of rules and regulations that would prevent enjoyment from rising to 'dangerous' levels.

Double Standards

The British view of nudity and sexuality has been coloured by the distorted religious teachings proclaimed over the last two thousand years. The ideals of the early Church, which depended on scripture for guidance in all matters, soon became diluted with the philosophies of those who became 'Christians' for reasons other than faith. Little by little Church teachings changed to a point where there were as many differences as similarities to the religion of the 1st century.[65]

---

[65] Augustine developed the concept of a 'Just War,' provided its purpose was noble and that love existed despite the necessary killing. His teachings were adopted and Christians remodelled themselves as 'Defenders of the Faith' as if God had changed his views on violence (Matthew 26:51-52). This move made possible not only the terrible Crusades, but it also empowered the clergy to preach the faithful into the trenches of the two bloodiest wars in history; the First and Second World War. Men returned from such conflicts convinced that if there was a God he did not care about mankind, thus Christendom's deviation from scripture damaged the faith of

Hung Out to Dry

Then here in England, a new development would escalate the situation, acting as a catalyst for the development of our unique culture of prudishness in the form of the British led *Industrial Revolution*.

Masses of country folk were attracted to the cities by the prospect of regular income and material gain. In the countryside the whole family would work together and family life provided a suitable environment for the upbringing of loving and responsible children. Crammed now into quickly built houses, family life was reshaped as all would work long hours in artificial and unhealthy conditions, separated from one another. Men and women would work 12 to 18 hours a day, wages were at starvation levels and child labour was commonplace. For the working classes, hard work and little pay took a heavy toll, especially when you consider the unsanitary condition of the slums they called home. The British had abolished slavery in 1833, but as Victoria ascended the throne just four years later, many of the working classes were living and working in conditions worse than those of the liberated slaves. The middle classes benefited greatly from the readily available cheap labour, with many amassing great fortunes. Life in the city bore no resemblance to the countryside paradise that the workers had left behind. Many workers would find escape through drink, but the seeds of discontent had been sown. The workers longed to escape from the dark drudgery of life. When release came, the workers rushed to enjoy it like a cork shooting from a bottle. But the middle classes felt a responsibility to moderate the behaviour of such 'roughs'.

By the Victorian era, restraint had become a cultural trait. The British were encouraged to shy away from showing their true feelings, focusing on duty and responsibility as they kept a 'stiff upper lip.' Emotions and sexual feelings were not expressed directly, but flowers[66] were used to send the message; thus retaining decorum and decency, separating people from the 'vulgarities' and earthiness of life. The Queen knew all too well how destructive the loose morals of the aristocracy had been in corroding people's respect for nobility and the Crown. Just two hundred years earlier, Oliver Cromwell had overthrown the monarchy, reintroducing Fundamentalist Christianity in a Puritan Republic.[67] When the monarchy was restored, loose living and debauchery returned, and by Victoria's reign, the disparity between the moral ideal and the vulgarity in which the people revelled, was all too obvious.

As missionaries trotted the globe in an effort to convert humanity, Euro-

---

generations, ultimately leading to its loss of power, influence and respect. (The film *Merry Christmas,* examines the 1914 truce through the eyes of French, Scottish, & German soldiers).
[66] Red roses symbolised passionate romantic love; pink - lesser affection, white flowers - virtue, yellow flowers - friendship.
[67] Christmas was abolished and pleasure seeking-condemned.

pean preachers went on to change not only the convert's religion but also his *culture*. The British Empire dominated the world, attempting to civilise it with teachings of Christian duty. Where native customs were retained (including minimal attire) many religionists viewed these so-called 'brothers in the faith' as little more than savages. Christianity and English culture came to symbolize the ideal in the minds of many representatives of the Church, and the view that the British way is God's way persists very much in Britain even today, being a carryover from our Empire days.

In distorting the thinking of their countrymen, the clergy overstepped the commandments of God. For centuries it was taught that water would recognise the righteous and envelop them should they enter it, whereas devils would float upon the surface as swimmers. Bible teachings on cleanliness were discarded as the Church taught its own ideas. Natural sexual desires became tainted as Church teachings brought feelings of shame and inhibition into marital relations. Godly women were not to enjoy such intimacies, rather they were to lie back and think of England until the beastly business was over. Once the family was established, the door closed to her affections, tempting husbands to look elsewhere. Yet double standards were evident everywhere, as even those promoting such ideologies were incapable of living by them. The British army at the Empire's front line were responsible for untold suffering. Seeking sexual gratification with native peoples, they spread venereal disease and sired countless children, whose skin colour alienated them from both British and native society. Many Catholic priests found that they could not live by the Church's rule of abstinence, resulting in the criminal abuse of countless children. Even though religionists have moderated their views and many have abandoned their faith, we are left with a paradox. The English find it quite acceptable on the one hand for men to acquire newspapers featuring photographs of women in various states of undress, but on the other hand, find the sight of a nursing mother quite unwholesome, especially if she feeds her baby in a public place such as a restaurant. This paradox results from our changed perception of the body. Even soft core pornography depicted in newspapers[68] encourages readers to view the body as sexual rather than natural. Thus, exposure of the breast in real life has become shocking; an opportunity for a nation of voyeurs to ogle. There is no wonder that mothers hide away.[69] Those who suffer with bowel problems or who discover lumps in their breast, often delay a visit to the doctor until it is too

---

[68] Tabloids such as *The Sun* introduced page 3 photographs of topless models in the 1970s.

[69] In our 'enlightened' times children are denied the immunological benefits of the breast in favour of the 'convenience' of the bottle. Children used to be fed by their mothers until they reached around five years, enjoying the warmth and security of maternal love and family bonding so lacking in today's frantic, career-led society.

late, and sadly 'die of embarrassment'. We British continue to pay a heavy price for all the social conditioning we have received. The middle classes took over from the Church to bring cultural changes that have shaped the nation. Yet all has not gone to plan, prudery has not led the people to the hoped-for safe harbours of moral excellence, rather it has resulted in moral decline and promiscuity with teachings of denial contributing to an accentuation of desire. The result is a society that has now become so sexualised that it is virtually impossible even for children to remain innocent. Broadband internet makes pornography readily available to all. Children as young as seven and most by the age of eleven satisfy their curiosity about sex with regular visits to the most depraved image sites they can find. With the nation's youngsters hooked on this diet of depravity, the façade of British prudery disguises a situation that rivals the decline of Roman society in seriousness. Despite our dysfunctional families, broken homes, disturbed, unsociable and, in many cases, amoral children, we continue in our confidence that the British way of life has no equal.

Although religious influence has nowadays receded, its power cannot just be turned off; rather its legacy echoes throughout our culture with the insistence on rules remaining evident everywhere. Unlike our European partners, we British are keen to do the right thing and especially to make sure that others do so. Particularly since the Industrial Revolution, we as a culture have felt it our duty to poke our nose into other people's business and take decision making out of their hands. We are told what to eat and drink, what to think and exactly how to bring up our children. The rules may change from week to week, but the nation follows in a game of 'Simon says' that has been played out for decades. We are frightened of doing the wrong thing and of expressing a different point of view. This has taken its toll on those eccentrics who have resisted the current tide, which is to view bathing in the great outdoors with suspicion. Gradually, towards the end of the last century, swimming in all but coastal waters has met with varying degrees of disapproval. Having discussed the powerful influence of religion on the ideas and attitudes of our nation, let us now look at another factor that has shaped the swimmer's fortune: the popularity of the seaside.

Chapter 3
Sex, Sea and Swimming Trunks

Oh, we do like to be beside the seaside, we do like to be beside the sea; yet the development of the seaside holiday would transform the swimmer's experience forever. Sea bathing was at one time a rarity, but those who swam in the sea did so without feeling any need to cover their nakedness. Men and boys in particular, enjoyed the freedom of the beach. But as the popularity of the seaside holiday increased, so did concern over public morals and hence costumes were insisted upon.

The reason for all of this is really quite complex and many factors have combined to influence the British cultural attitude towards what is and is not acceptable on the beach. The seaside holiday was after all a uniquely British 'invention', and so it was up to the British to decide on the subject of propriety. This chapter outlines the evolution of the seaside, and the telling effect this would have upon the swimmer.

The Fountain of Health

As the benefits of cold-water bathing became publicised, initially it was the 'well-to-do' that benefitted from the profusion of inland spas. Hydrotherapy was considered to be of great benefit as a health cure. The purity of the water led to its consumption in great quantity, despite the often unpleasant taste resulting from the heavy concentration of minerals. The health cure usually included immersion in cold water on a regular basis throughout one's stay at the resort. Appropriate spas would be recommended as medicines, matching the patient's ailments with the chemical composition of the waters. With the wide selection of spas available, all manner of illnesses were matched to the curative waters of one or more spas. England was blessed with a few hot water springs (sadly some have been lost in recent times), the most popular being situated in Bath. In stark contrast to many of its rivals, Bath's waters were and still are very warm indeed. Although you might think that Bath alone would have succeeded as a health resort, it was in fact cold-water bathing that the doctor preferred. Before long, advantage was taken of the copious amount of cold salty water that surrounds the British Isles. Hence the fashion for 'taking the waters' quickly extended to the coast - at least for the rich. Poor people on the other hand had to make the best of what they could afford. A large number of wells dotted all

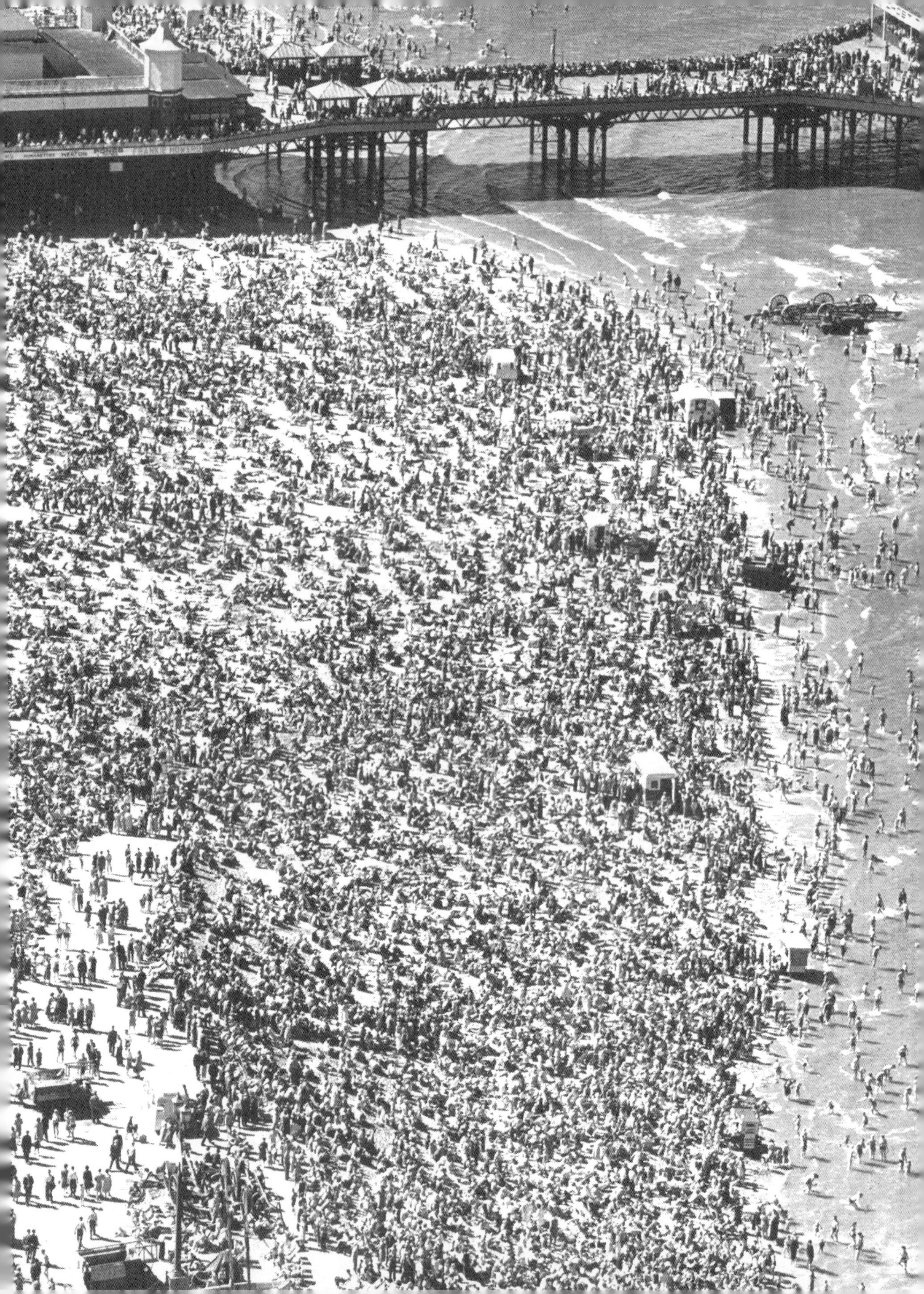
HEATON

Sex, Sea and Swimming Trunks

Opposite: Crowds fill the beach at Blackpool July 1949.

over the kingdom became the poor man's spa. Some of these wells remain today, and in Cornwall people have continued the tradition of tying clouties[70] (small pieces of cloth taken from a garment worn over an ailment), to trees and bushes growing nearby. They believe that as the material disintegrates and drops into the water, so their prayers will be answered and the illness of the ailing one will depart. Thus, a legacy from wishing well times benefited the poorer public, who simply could not afford the luxury of repeated or extended visits to such wells. They left their clouties, in order that they might magically benefit from the waters even though absent in the flesh.

The wealthy who had time on their hands needed transport to enable them to reach the spas and at about this time Thomas Cook of Leicester was just beginning to establish his now world famous excursion firm. It began with a special train from Leicester to Loughborough for a temperance meeting in 1841. This, it is believed, was the first publicly advertised train excursion in England. Midland Counties Railways were the first to put on trains for tours organised by Cook. His first commercial excursion ran to Liverpool in 1845. This four-day trip was hugely popular; twelve hundred first and second-class passengers filled the train and demand was so great that he ran a second train four weeks later. Soon he was advertising trips to Scarborough, offering attractions such as steamboat trips to nearby Whitby and Bridlington, two mineral spas and sea bathing.[71] Within just twenty years, Cook had developed his network extensively, organising trips for the rich to America and to the Nile. For the poor, day trips by train were laid on and cheap day returns meant that more could get away. The third class transport amounted to nothing more that a place in an open wagon and

Thomas Cook of Leicester

---

[70] A Cornish word for cloth.
[71] The first seaside excursion ran in 1843 devised by Sir Rowland Hill; according to Anthony Hern's book: *The Seaside Holiday*.

Hung Out to Dry

one's having to be prepared to accept all that the weather and, more perilously, the steam engine might throw at you. The travellers were undeterred, they were getting away and that's what mattered. Thomas Cook holidays are respected worldwide as a major player in the holiday business even today.

In this 21st century, the thought of bathing in cold water might seem quite abhorrent. However, the benefits of doing so remain. Recent research shows that a daily cold-water bath raises significantly one's resistance to disease and, much as we now enjoy the hot tub, we cannot deny that the after effects leave us feeling drowsy. In sharp contrast, the cold-water bath both enlivens and invigorates. Those who are used to cold-water bathing find the resultant feelings of afterglow and well-being somewhat addictive, and for this reason the dawn swim continues in many places even today. Our ancestors were very well aware of these benefits and naturally the winter months were seen as the healthiest of all. Interestingly, cold-water bathing was sought out not only by the nation's hardy men and boys; the fact is that quite a number of the fairer sex enjoyed cold water bathing when they could, despite the risk of exposure:

The four and twentieth day of May
Of all times of the-year,
A Virgin lady bright and gay
Did privately appear.

Close by the riverside which she
Did single out the rather,
'Cause she was sure it was secure
And had intend to bathe her.

With glittering glance, her jealous eyes
Did slyly look about.
To see if any lurking spies
Were hid to find her out.

And being well resolved that none
Could view her nakedness.
She put her robes off one by one,
And doth her-self undress.

The swimming Lady – anon – late 17th Century[72]

---

[72] Cunnington & Mansfield: *English Costume for Sports and Outdoor Recreation.*

Just for Fun

In July 1847, we find Queen Victoria driving to the beach to enjoy bathing in the seawater for the first time. This visit is of special interest to us. She was not of course the first Monarch to visit the seaside, George III bathed at Weymouth and George IV at Brighton; but, in a manner that seems quite out of character, Queen Victoria could be said to be the first monarch to have bathed for *pleasure* as opposed to *health*. This marked a change, in that seaside places were beginning to evolve from the status of health spas into pleasure resorts.

The transformation was often quite dramatic and sudden. Clacton-on-Sea is a good example. Back in the 1870s, Clacton was somewhat insignificant. But by the 1890s it had grown from an inconsequential mark on the map, to a bustling seaside town with a pavilion and a pier some 1,180 feet long. The same can be said for what was once known as Bourne Bottom. Once an isolated, uninhabited heath land, it was transformed by the arrival in 1810 of Captain Lewis Tregonwell and his wife Henrietta. They fell in love with the place and built a seaside mansion (now part of the Royal Exeter Hotel), others did the same and by 1856 it proudly presented its first pier (replaced by the ancestor of the current structure in 1861). By the end of the 19th century Bourne Bottom had become the country's top resort, now more suitably named Bournemouth!

Piers were a very important part of the scene. The first to be built was at Southend-on-Sea in 1830. It was rammed six times by ships, eventually being rebuilt in 1889. During the 1890s, it was extended repeatedly until eventually it reached out into the sea some 7,080 feet, making it the longest pleasure pier in the world.

Middle class people in particular enjoyed strolling along the piers of England, imagining themselves at sea aboard a luxury liner just as though they were part of the upper class. Even the way they dressed added to the illusion and helped them to imitate their 'betters'. Thus the pier and the promenade established themselves as essential holiday amenities.

The desire of holidaymakers to feel good about themselves led to the introduction of 'The Visitor Book' into hotels and guesthouses. In Southport, for example, the local newspaper was actually called: *The Visitor*. Snobbery was thus encouraged, as holidaymakers kept watch for those with status staying at the resort. People delighted to boast about those with whom they had holidayed, even if in reality this only amounted to a passing glance.

At first the working classes visited only for the day, travelling from nearby towns, mostly by train. From London though, you could travel by steamship to Margate Hoy and many did, docking at the pier of their holiday destination. By 1900 the middle classes were spending between one and two

Hung Out to Dry

weeks by the sea. The connection between one's status and one's holiday was thus established and has continued for the last hundred years.

For working class people the seaside held a great attraction. Having been pulled into the towns by the magnetism of the Industrial Revolution, they longed for the freedom of the countryside that they could so well remember. A day trip to the coast was in sharp contrast to the squalid conditions they had to endure on a daily basis back home.[73] A day by the sea was in effect an escape from everyday reality and the sense of release and excitement was very evident. Working class people were less sophisticated than those who viewed themselves as their betters. Their behaviour often shocked because they were so much more open about sexuality than the upper classes. The beach proved to be a great amusement to these visitors. Concert parties didn't start until mid-afternoon, so young couples entertained themselves on the beach, their displays of affection being another cause for concern.

'Pray excuse me madam, my bathing-machine I think!'

---

[73] The first Bank Holiday was instituted in 1871.

Sex, Sea and Swimming Trunks

There was also plenty to see near the bathing machines. Men, regardless of class, found the prospect of seeing scantily clad or even naked ladies (as was the case in the early days), descending into the sea from their bathing machines quite irresistible. Even when costumes were worn, they would cling when wet and many became transparent. On the whole, ladies came to bathe rather than to swim and they especially enjoyed having the waves wash over them as they lay in the shallows. The waves would wash their dresses up, exposing even more to the spectators. For the sake of appearances a telescope enabled 'gentlemen' to keep a discreet distance. Many seaside councils capitalised on this and found a good way to make a few pennies out of visitors by providing telescopes for public use, despite the fact that 'peeping Toms' were officially disapproved of.

The atmosphere of freedom on the beach was reflected in the profusion of postcards featuring sexual humour. Working class visitors proved very receptive to these naughty postcards. Conversely, the prudish middle classes began to seek out quieter places, with some even travelling abroad to escape association with the 'riff raff.'

Visitors to the seaside came at first to partake of the waters, in much the same way as did visitors to the health spas. This meant that people were coming to bathe in the sea, rather than to swim. Most simply wanted to paddle at the water's edge and this led to a conflict of interest between the two groups. Paddlers could simply slip off their shoes and roll up their trousers or lift their skirts, whereas swimmers insisted on swimming in the nude, with bathers coming somewhere in-between. Today we see the seaside holiday as an opportunity to sunbathe but this was not part of the experience in these early days. Daytrippers did not want to waste their time queuing up for bathing machines, but preferred to enjoy themselves exuberantly on the water's edge.

The bathing machine provided the 'respectable' lady with a means of privately undressing, whilst being transported to waters deep enough to cover her nakedness. This shed on wheels was not of course ideal as things were rather rushed. After waiting her turn to use the machine she would find a soggy dark interior in which she was expected to change, even though the machine was in motion, bumping and jolting over the sand and into the shallows. The seaward doors were then flung open and she was expected to immediately descend the steps in full view of the assembled audience. It is amusing to think of these poor women being torn between the desire to have their nakedness covered by the seawater and their reluctance to plunge into the cold restlessness of their ally. Additionally, the pressure from the bathing attendant to hurry things up was often vocalised as they were very anxious to accommodate as many customers as possible each day. Waiting rooms were full and so many adventurers were more or less pushed into the briny by these attendants to speed things

Hung Out to Dry

along. On returning to the machine, our lady would find the floor awash with salt water, a sight that proved less than welcoming as a changing surface. The doors would close tight behind her and she would then try to dry and dress herself as the 'shed' lurched back up the sand behind its horse.

MERMAIDS at BRIGHTON

This was a very British way of going on. The palaver proved to be of great amusement to those of the working class who had little access to privacy back home, let alone on the beach. Many of the poorly built slums in which they lived included toilets with open shared facilities. Members of both sexes were well used to seeing each other performing the most private of functions. One of the attractions for these workers in visiting the seaside was to witness this amusing spectacle, and the fact that they were on hand to watch it made the whole process pointless anyway!

The first bathing machines appeared in Scarborough and Margate. Later, modesty hoods were added to prevent the users being exposed as they descended the steps into the sea. By the early 19th century, men were also expected to use these contraptions and as you can imagine, this did not go down at all well.

Indecent Exposure

Throughout history, English men had bathed naked outdoors whether in river pond or sea. Women also bathed likewise until the early 1800s. But those who wanted to preserve decency objected to its continuance. On the whole women bathed, but the men both bathed *and* swam. Men though resisted the notion of covering themselves as they considered bathing outfits both unnecessary and dangerously restrictive. They had openly enjoyed bathing in the nude until the 1830s, and it continued less openly until the 1870s.[74]

By the 1850s the joy of a man's being able to strip on the beach and rush into the sea was constrained to certain out of the way places and then only at certain times. Even these restrictions did not prove sufficient to quell the complaints of the gentry. *The Scarborough Gazette* in 1866 reported:

> *'Hundreds of men and women may be seen in the water, the men stark naked and the women so loosely and insufficiently clad that for all purposes of decency they might as well have been naked too.'*

Over in France mixed bathing had established itself. Here in England, despite the fact that men did not want to bathe with women, the French influence gradually took over and so the time had come to face the question of bathing costumes. For the middle classes, who were very anxious to be seen to be doing the right thing during their seaside holiday, the trend towards beachwear was readily adopted.[75]

Bathing Machines at Brighton: notice the men changing in the open.

---

[74] Cunnington & Mansfield: *English Costume for Sports and Outdoor Recreation* 1969.
[75] Cyril Bainbridge: *Pavilions on the sea*.

Hung Out to Dry

The whole idea of the bathing machine was to allow nude bathing to continue with decency. But the advent of mixed bathing and bathing drawers forced these cumbersome devises into semi-retirement. Here enters the wheel-less bathing machine still evident all around the British coast and known today as 'The Beach Hut'.

The 1830s saw the beginning of swimming races in Europe. The British Swimming Club held its first race in 1861 and all competitors were warned that they would not be allowed to compete unless they wore swimming drawers. Such views were not held by everyone however, as the letters and memoirs of Sir William Hardman 1863 record:

> *'Rather let the preposterous exhibition of our bather go on, than condemn the Briton rushing into his native sea to feel instead of the vigorous hug of Neptune, a clammy clutch from shoulder to knee... but let us have none of your damp, unpleasant garments.'*

The experience of Parson Kilverts illustrates the displeasure of many a gent who would have preferred that things had not changed (1874).

> *'At Shanklin one has to adopt the detestable custom of bathing in drawers. If ladies don't like to see men naked why don't they keep away from the sight? Today I had a pair of drawers given me, which I could not keep on. The rough waves stripped them off and tore them down by my ankles. Whilst thus fettered I was seized and flung down by a heavy sea, which retreating suddenly left me lying naked on the sharp shingle from which I rose streaming with blood. After this I took the wretched and dangerous rag off and of course there were some ladies looking on as I came out of the water.'*

In 1882 nude bathing obviously continued, as shown by the fact that a notice on indecent bathing (Borough of Colchester) was felt necessary, it read:

> *'No person shall bathe from the highway, street, or public place without wearing drawers or such other dress covering as to prevent indecent exposure.'*

Also a letter in *The Swimming Magazine* 1st March 1884 expressed this opinion:

> *'Would proprietors of baths compel their patrons to wear drawers during the forthcoming season? I am not over-particular, but I think the practice should extend to boys, particularly precocious ones.'*

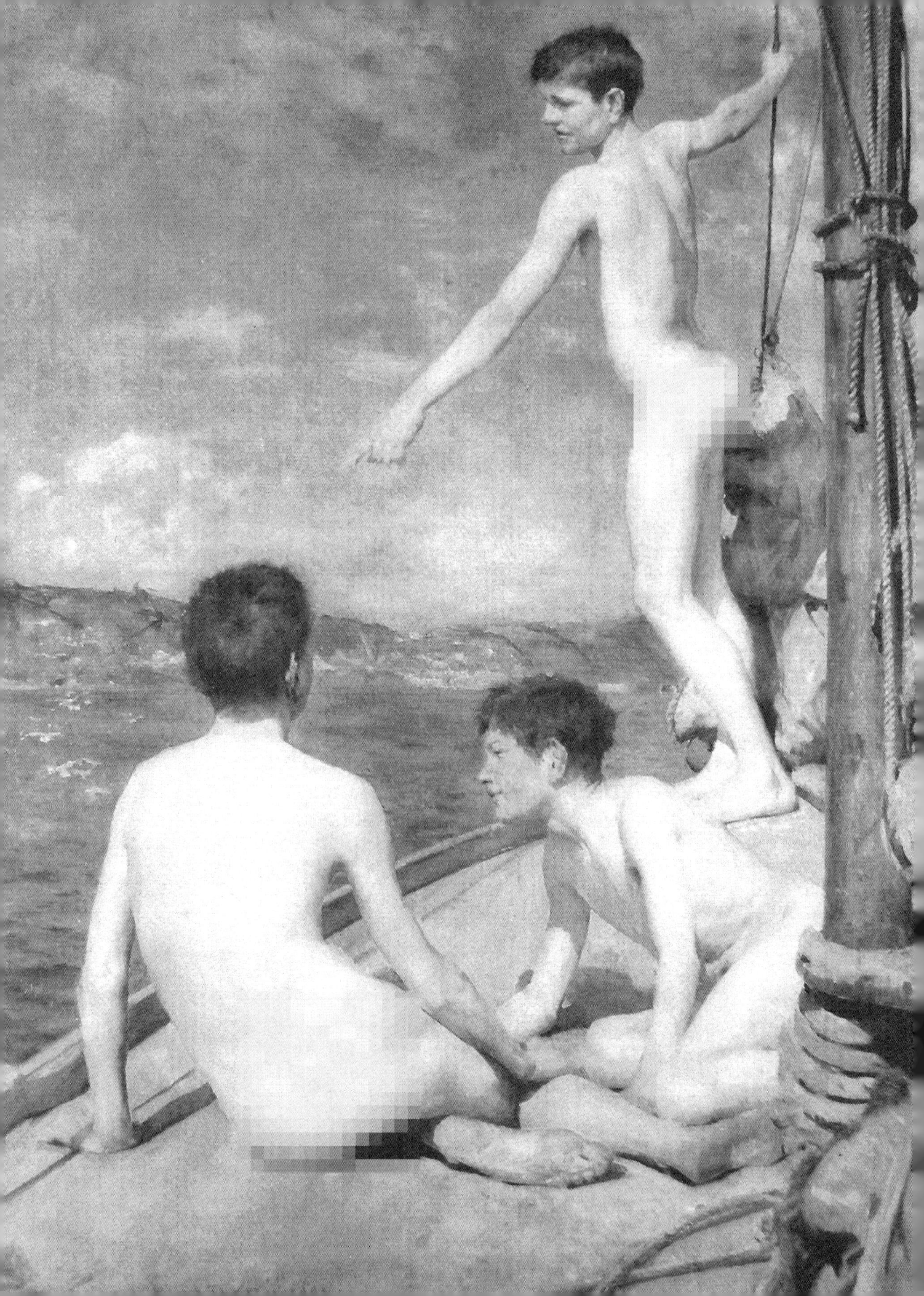

The End of Innocence

Meanwhile down in Falmouth Cornwall, Henry Scott Tuke (1858-1929) was busying himself painting the scene of naked boys bathing, in an effort, as he said in an 1895 interview, to capture the *'truth and beauty of flesh in the sunlight by the sea.'*

Bathers (pictured on the previous page) is perhaps one of Tuke's best paintings and takes pride of place at the foot of the staircase in Leeds Art Gallery. It was first exhibited by the New English Art Club in 1889. Tuke, by no means the only artist who endeavoured to preserve the appealing image of naked bathers, captured the imagination of the middle classes and agreeably pictured for them the freedom and innocence of boyhood. Times were changing and personal freedoms were being eroded. Many artists and photographers likewise produced similar works at around this time, but nowadays with our changed perception of child nudity concerns have been raised as to the painter's interest in his subject matter. Many are very defensive of Tuke and explain away any concerns by saying that he merely painted what he saw. There is an element of truth in such reasoning, but it has to be said that after examining the work of artists in other media (who also portrayed 'what they saw', including agreeable depictions of nude bathers), that their portfolios are not as densely saturated with such images as is the case with Tuke. In fact, Tuke painted so many bathing pictures that they came to be his trademark and his depictions a cause of some amusement in that his pictures varied so little. However Tuke's private life is not my concern here, there is certainly no hint of scandal connected with *his* actions; rather, it is the very fact that public displays of his work were the cause of so much consternation. Many felt uncomfortable with his subject, whilst at the same time they could not deny his artistic talent and success. Public concern over the sexuality of children and particularly boys brought forth sweeping changes for British culture. Two years after the appearance of Tuke's *Bathers* the Amateur Swimming Association ruled: *'Henceforth bathing drawers must be worn for all bathing events.'* This meant that boys would now have to follow in the footsteps of their elders and that their freedom was to come to an end.

The social structure that had been so well ordered prior to the Industrial Revolution was by now in a state of metamorphosis, a process that saw the nation churn in an endless fermentation that seems to be restarted with every wind of change. The upper classes were being thrust into confrontation with the ways and manners of the workers and this caused a series of conflicts, and these conflicts brought change, albeit little by little. Although the working classes didn't bother with bathing machines on the beach, it wasn't until the early 1900s that a

Sex, Sea and Swimming Trunks

'respectable' woman could be seen strolling along the beach in her coverall costume, but it did ultimately prove acceptable.

For men, swimming drawers or calecons were now obligatory. The law on mixed bathing changed in 1901 and so the calecon went on to develop still further into a costume that would cover the upper body and shoulders as decency became ever more important. By this time mixed bathing was well established and the bathing machines were enjoying their retirement at many resorts. Bathing tents were brought in to replace them, thus galvanizing the British obsession with 'decency' on the beach.

Boys, of course, continued to bathe unclothed and many photographs and postcards are testament to this fact. For a time at least, boys were left to enjoy the pleasure of their natural state, either in public school or in the river, if not at the seaside.

Attitudes Change

Working class boys had little chance of privacy even at home. They usually slept unclothed, sharing a bed with their siblings and an outside lavatory with the whole of the local neighbourhood. Joseph Dare, a Leicester evangelist, reported that fifteen families shared just one lavatory situated in the rear courtyard and in full view.

Where improved sanitation existed, a collection of between two to eight seats would fill the chamber with no partitioning. Boys would commonly urinate in the street and enjoyed doing so; upon leaving the cinema, boys would congregate just outside and discharge a steaming river that would rush down the street. By 1950 only 46% of British households had a bathroom. Boys were used to bathing in a tin bath either in the kitchen or in front of the fire; there was no room for privacy. It was not at all unusual for neighbours to call by on bath days; so it is not surprising that these boys were in no hurry to hide what everyone had already seen many times before.

Even the well-to-do could see nothing wrong with skinny-dipping. In fact, young gentlemen from Oxford and Cambridge delighted in the lack of restrictions. At the school of Eton,[76] boys bathing, even in the main river, did not wear costumes until 1895; adult males having swam similarly up until about the

---

[76] Frank Sachs: *The Complete Swimmer* 1912.

Hung Out to Dry

1870s. Male nudity was not seen as in any way erotic or shameful, whereas female nakedness, even to the slightest extent, was seen as entirely improper. However by 1920, boys older than ten were expected to dress decently. This was of course impractical for those who were too poor to possess undergarments. Many would simply tie a rag around their waist to appease the ruling classes, although this did little to protect their modesty. Boys bathing spontaneously in the river did so in the costume of Eden until at least the end of the Second World War. At the seaside, bathing costumes and towels were customarily hired out up until the eve of the war; these black, baggy and shapeless outfits came in just three sizes and all inscribed with the Corporation logo to prevent pilfering. At Leicester's two bathing stations, the Corporation costumes were constantly being mutilated, with the effect that issue was restricted to mixed bathing days, so again liberty to bathe 'au naturel' was to survive a little longer.

Room for all!

During the Second World War costumes became impossible to obtain. They were not considered essential to the war effort and so as stocks became depleted, responsibility for decency shifted from Corporation control into the hands of the general public. The individual bather would now have to provide his own covering. This change ultimately led to the development of much more suitable attire from the swimmers point of view. Knitted costumes suddenly became common; knitting patterns were sold to industrious mothers keen to provide essential covering for their sons, but their offspring were not so keen on the idea. When wet, such garments became incredibly heavy and were soon discarded in favour of nature. Mothers were appeased by the covert dipping of such costumes in water prior to home time. Woe betide any boy that forgot the means of his deception.[77] The control of the swimming public, however, was now very much on the minds of local and national governments.

Holidays in the Sun

As if out of nowhere sunbathing suddenly rose to popularity; a good suntan became the symbol of excellent health, and the hot summer of 1928 started the fashion of being sunburnt. Gymnosophists (or Naturists as they are now known) were to be marginalized by the press. But the nation as a whole came to see semi-nude sunbathing as a very good thing. Thus, pressure was exerted by those who wanted to sunbathe in public for permission to uncover more and more flesh. At the Lido in Hyde Park, men started pulling down their one piece costumes to the waist, but the police took a very dim view of this and firmly reinforced the dress code for the sake of decency, law and order.

The upper classes were now holidaying abroad, leaving the middle classes to the hotels around the coast, but where were the workers to stay? Initially they found accommodation in boarding houses, but this meant holidaymakers had to walk the streets during the day whatever the weather, and if it rained, as often it did, a miserable holiday was to be endured with fortitude.[78] More suitable arrangements were just on the horizon; prior to World War II over 200 holiday camps opened their doors. The working classes responded with unbounded enthusiasm, and the seaside holiday camp era established itself immediately. Billy Butlin who provided *'a week's holiday for a week's wage'*, opened his first camp at Skegness in 1936. Butlin's holidays went on to offer not just dancing and community sports activities, but also indoor and outdoor swimming pools with fortified glass, allowing spectators to see the legs of the swimmers, a real novelty in its day. Additionally, funfair rides, table tennis, snooker, boat hire, zoos, theatres, picture houses, roller-skating, cable-cars, miniature trains and real steam engines to climb on, all added to the sense of excitement and wonder.[79] Working class children found themselves transported into a paradise of independence and abundance. If they needed help, all they had to do was ask a Redcoat. It was 'fun, fun, fun', and more importantly for such poverty stricken families, parents did not have to say no, as everything

---

[77] Richard Rutt: *The Englishman's Swimwear* 1990 (Costume).
[78] Miriam Akhtar & Steve Humphries: *Some liked it Hot*.
[79] Pwllheli - North Wales.

Hung Out to Dry

was free! The problem of what to do during bad weather was solved at once!

The social changes brought by the war meant that even the middle classes frequented these camps for a while. But the package holiday to Spain was just around the corner, followed by more exotic destinations, which ultimately spelled the end of the holiday camp era and even the end for British resorts as a whole. The working classes found that they could now afford to travel abroad, as it was often cheaper to fly to the sun than to stay in a hotel in the damp of England.

By now many of the seaside cafés, once so popular, were looking pathetically empty. Visitors were no longer looking for the coldest bathing in the country, but would visit the coast only during the height of the summer; a season of not much more than six weeks. However, the popularity of the seaside had, in its boom, been responsible for the introduction of swimwear. But the rising standards of living and the shortening of the season now that sunbathing became part of the experience, meant that British resorts could no longer afford to satisfy the demands of the holidaying public, who in any case preferred the prestige of travelling abroad.

Towards the end of the 20th century ideas were again changing. The medical profession, having introduced sunbathing to improve the health of the

Ramsgate sands accommodate thousands keen on sun, sea and fresh air.

population, now did an about-turn as it re-invented the sun as foe rather than friend. Those once healthful rays were vilified as the basis for a dramatic rise in the incidence of skin cancer. Rather than weigh the benefits against the risks, the sun was to be outlawed, casting a shadow over those that loved to lie out in its warmth. Yet, in our green and pleasant land with its absence of rays for months on end, is there is any wonder that we take advantage of the sun whenever it shines? The sun lifts our mood, resurrecting us from our winter blues. No wonder we British are known worldwide for our sunshine fascination as we fry our flesh in the scorching heat whenever the sun comes out.

The fashion in swimwear continues to change. As sun exposure becomes less fashionable, there has been a move to keep - children in particular - more or less completely covered, even on the beach. Working class children have experienced a dramatic rise in their standard of living. Most sleep in a bed of their own, if not their own room. They enjoy the comfort of indoor private bathing and toilet facilities, not to mention central heating and double-glazing. The reduction in family size means that children enjoy greater privacy and many are now very self-conscious when it comes to their appearance and image. Advertising and the media encourage all to reach out for bodily perfection through the use of various products and preparations. Boys spend hours in front of the mirror tending to their hair and girls as young as eight are suffering from anorexia as they diet for fashion. There is great anxiety over body image and so interest in designer clothing and accessories lead the British to spend a fortune on their appearance. This anxiety shows itself on the beach and at the swimming pool. Children may still enjoy an illicit swim in either the canal or lake, but always clothed, if not fully clothed. On the beach children bathe in wet suits to protect them from the cold, having become accustomed to a more pampered way of life.

Swimmers originally complained that the wearing of a costume was detrimental to speed, and it even became fashionable for competitors to shave off their body hair and with it see depletion in their swimming times. Now at the Olympic Games, we see competitors wear Lycra coveralls to elevate their speed, a fashion that makes Victorian costumes look skimpy indeed! Has the desire to cover up improved public morals? Apparently not; reports about paedophiles and their exploitation of children abound in the British press, giving all the more reason to protect children from the gaze of those who might hurt them. Even so, the UK sports the highest rate of teenage pregnancies in Western Europe. The nation as a whole finds the subject of sexuality too embarrassing to discuss without awkwardness. Sex and guilt are now part of the fabric of British culture, the words nude and rude being likewise inseparable yet the nation has developed an obsession with sex. Despite all efforts to arrest the trend, sexually transmitted diseases have reached epidemic proportions, abortions are commonplace and broken homes are becoming the rule rather than the exception.

Another change at the swimming baths has been the departure from the changing cubicle into more open plan changing areas, for the men at least. This resulted from fear as to what may have been going on in secret. These changes were much to the consternation of the junior public, who had only just got used to the idea that they needed to hide themselves away, when the screen of privacy was stripped from around them. The latest development has seen a move towards the 'changing village'. Cubicles for use by both sexes are provided in the same area, inevitably encouraging all kinds of ingenuity for those unable to resist a peek on their neighbours. On the continent things are very different. At many pools in Germany, Switzerland and Scandinavia, a swimmer will be given a bar of soap and is expected to strip shower before entering the pool, in order to keep the water clean. Diagrams on the wall leave one in no doubt as to exactly what is to be washed and how. The English equivalent is a quick dash through the foot shower, which you will agree, is more 'modest' in every way. Instead of washing ourselves before we swim, we swim in disinfectant, confident that the British way is best of all.

In conclusion, it would appear that the fashion to wear clothes whilst swimming in England is here to stay. Swimwear may be a comparatively new invention, but the last 150 years has seen our view of it change from abhorrence in the beginning, to seeing it as absolutely essential today. At the beginning of the new millennium we find that child nudity has become taboo. Senior schoolboys were once trained in the use of public showers as all had to shower nude with no exceptions (up until the early 1980s).[80] This was seen as important, to help boys overcome childish embarrassment and bodily shame. After all there was no room for bashfulness should boys enter the Forces or the mines. Baden Powell encouraged twice daily exercise for scouts who were to wear: 'little or no clothing.' Today, though, a chasm exists between our attitudes and those of the past; even showering is rare at some schools as the need for privacy supercedes the need to wash.

Despite improvements in living conditions throughout Europe, attitudes have developed quite differently outside of Britain. German culture lacks the prudishness that we in Britain have fostered for so long. On Danish beaches nude bathing is still commonplace, just as was the case on British beaches before the seaside fashion. The sauna culture of the Finns tolerates family nudity but lacks the immorality that we British might fear. We here in England are still

---

[80] To see just how attitudes have changed, the film *Kes* is something of a time capsule (1970). In some schools nude swimming was also compulsory for boys up until the early 1980s.

Sex, Sea and Swimming Trunks

feeling the effects of our religious heritage (as discussed in the previous chapter). Added to this, the many rules imposed by the middle classes have not only set the seeds of change, they have blossomed into a national obsession.

The misery of bathing in drawers 1898. Master Tommy is emphatically of the opinion that the sexes should *not* bathe together!

Hung Out to Dry

We may now appreciate how a nation of skinny-dippers came to cover up, encouraged by the middle classes during the Industrial Revolution. We better understand why rules and regulations are such a part of the British psyche, but this still does not fully explain our current obsession with prudery. To understand this, we must consider another development: the science of sunbathing. Again you may wonder at the connection between sunshine and the swimmer, but by reading the next two chapters you will discover how an eagerness to get into the sun, ultimately put the swimmer into the shade.

The Horse and Jockey! This diving formation, once common in pools all over the country, has fallen by the wayside. When the divers reached the water, the jockey would lie back, diving feet first.

Chapter 4
Sunny Days, Dark Shadows

Mad dogs and Englishmen lie out in the midday sun. We English really have made a name for ourselves with our eccentricities in modern times. But sunbathing, of course, predates our experimentation with it. Today fears over skin cancer have changed our view of a sun kissed skin, but such has not always been the case.

Early Days

The Egyptians enjoyed many health benefits by exposing their skin to the sun. Children in Egypt often wore little until they approached puberty and male slaves wore only a loincloth as covering. As the nation moved through history, fashions changed to the point that in later years only the lower classes would expose the torso, but without doubt, the nation worshiped the sun!

In Rome, practically every home had its solarium or sun parlour. Art and history reveal that both the Greeks and Romans were relaxed about nakedness. The Greek Games saw male runners and gymnasts compete unclothed and this was seen as totally appropriate (though females were not permitted as spectators). Greek boys from eight to eighteen years would daily attend the gymnasium - an open air sports ground - at which they would perform their exercises stark naked to musical accompaniment. Interestingly, swimming was not included with the games of the Panathenaic Festival; rather it was reserved for pleasure and refreshment. In later years, swimming pools were added to many gymnasiums to complement the baths that predated them.

Trouble in Eden

Regardless of our personal views on the matter of faith, one cannot deny that our ancestors held very strongly to the notion that the Bible is the Word of God. By examining these ancient writings and the way in which they were perceived, we open for ourselves an opportunity to better understand the formation of our culture. For example, the Bible in its first book relates that after disobeying God, the originally naked Adam and Eve hid themselves and covered their genitals. The shame felt by this first couple was to be misconstrued by Jerome and Augustine to have stemmed from lust and sexual sin. Thus, the Church came to view nudity and immorality as synonymous. Interestingly though, baptism in those early days took place with the convert in a state of nature.[81] This is not to suggest that God somehow favoured the naked state; people were just more relaxed about nudity then than we are today. Baptism symbolised rebirth, as the initiate rose from the waters he was born anew and nudity symbolised this new beginning.[82] Additionally, Christian converts came in the main from the lower echelons of society; their wardrobe lacked bathing garments which would have been seen as quite unnecessary. The newly baptised immediately redressed, putting on a white garment to symbolise purity.

The Bible does not condemn nakedness, but it does show that clothing was to be worn once mankind left the Garden of Eden. Interestingly, it says that Eve was the first to eat of the forbidden fruit when on her own and yet she felt no shame as a result. Later Adam joined her in sin and the account goes on to show that gradually they began to comprehend the gravity of what they had done. Realising that their offspring would suffer as a result, the first couple developed feelings of shame and covered their genitals.[83] Despite this, it would seem that bodily shame is not inherent in mankind, rather it is a learnt behaviour acquired from one's parents, peers or community. When such shame is absent, it can still be developed if outsiders insist on bestowing their attitudes onto others.

The prophets of Bible times are shown to have occasionally exhibited unusual behaviour at God's direction, by going naked in what might otherwise be considered inappropriate circumstances. Their nakedness either illustrated humility or prophesied humiliation. Such was the case with Isaiah who went naked for three years.[84] The Bible's description of the Shulammite maiden in the *Song of Solomon* and the Law Covenant's open and frank discussion of sexuality, are but two examples of its un-British candour when dealing with sexual matters. Those who read the Bible for themselves are soon persuaded that God is *not* an Englishman. This becomes a hard pill to swallow for those who have been brought up in the West. Western art has for years depicted Jesus, the Son of God, as a fair-haired blue eyed European, whereas we know he

---

[81] Peter Partner: *Two Thousand Years the First Millennium – The Birth of Christianity to the Crusades.*
[82] Robin Margaret Jensen: *Understanding early Christian art.*
[83] God had expressly warned Adam that if he ate from the tree of the 'Knowledge of Good and Bad' he would die. Through his rebellion, Adam cut himself off from his Creator, and thus sentenced his future offspring to imperfection and ultimately death. Having cut the umbilical cord to life he could not pass on perfection to his descendants. Adam and Eve damaged the future prospects for mankind and so hid their genitals of which they were now ashamed; Romans 5:12.
[84] The term naked can also imply scantily clad. Micah 1:8-11, I Samuel 19:24, Isaiah 20:2-4.

was a Jew with Jewish features, no doubt dark hair, brown eyes and olive skin. Add to this the tendency to read history backwards (looking at events and customs from our 'enlightened' standpoint through a veil of preconceptions), and misunderstandings are inevitable. For the sake of 'decency' then, the exodus from Egypt is usually depicted with the children wearing 'suitable' attire, whereas in fact Egyptian children often wore little in summer, let alone the children of slaves.[85] This is not to suggest that the Israelites experienced nudity in the same way as the Romans and Greeks. Even so, they were not taught to be *prudish*. No objection was voiced in the Bible against swimming and bathing, or against competing in the games where male runners sped along after putting off every weight,[86] including their garments. However, the scene of the world changed dramatically during the first half of the first millennium as Church doctrine superseded Bible teaching.

British Culture

Cultures around the world have developed quite different attitudes toward the naked state. Those that experience it as their daily attire do not see it as immodest or as in any way sexual, but rather, the *wearing* of clothes is viewed with suspicion. We have seen that some of our European neighbours still have quite an open and tolerant attitude towards nudity. An example of this is illustrated by an account I read of a German swimmer, who having enjoyed his swim down a river in the park wearing only his 'birthday suit', decided to take public transport for the return trip to his clothing. Officials objected to his travel, not because of his lack of attire, but because of his excuse; the swimmer said that he could not be expected to carry money due to his naked state! In the end he travelled freely and this in the truest sense of the word! In considering this experience, our reaction to it reveals just how British we are. Despite the fact that we might wish to be open minded and tolerant, we find that our upbringing and social conditioning cause us to respond automatically with shock, amusement or embarrassment.

At the seaside we are accustomed to buying sticks of rock with the name of the holiday town running right through its centre. Interestingly, the British today hold a similar trait. Regardless of the fact that we might try to convince ourselves otherwise, we are British through and through. The seaside shaped our culture and so in a sense the stick of rock symbolises the end product of its

---

[85] Before leaving Egypt the sons of Israel were bestowed with many gifts including much in the way of clothing, however customs would not have changed overnight.
[86] 1 Corinthians 9:24-25, Hebrews 12:1.

effects; we as a nation are British to the core. The British are the product of control; we like to control others and to be in control ourselves. A look or a sigh is often enough to convey our disapproval.

The seaside holiday may have developed here in England, but the countries of Europe and America were soon to follow suit. As the fashion extended, so the British trademark of propriety was to be spread abroad, seeding change in other cultures. Bernard Falk in his book: *He Laughed in Fleet Street* (1933), recounts his experience:

> *'When I arrived nude sea-bathing, common to most parts of Russia, was in full swing. Fathers and mothers marched into the water with their families, blissfully unconscious of any sense of awkwardness. Whether for sea bathing or sunbathing, the fully - exposed human form presented no hindrance to social life. But the advent of the allied troops caused a subtle difference in the attitude of women bathers. With true, coquettish instinct, they took to stylish bathing dresses.'*

The British led the rest of the world to question 'freedom' on the beach. On the Black Sea back in the 1920s, bathers saw no need for costumes. That is, until pressure came to bear from European tourists. The influence of these visitors meant that traditionalists found themselves restricted to a few small areas; they were hidden out of the way, so as not to bring the disapproval of the newcomers. Likewise, thirty years ago, East German sunbathers using the beaches around the Darss Peninsula outnumbered costume-clad bathers six to one, but predictably the advance of condemnatory tourists is forcing cultural change.

The British Empire once dominated the world, being confident of its superiority. As a nation we came to see nudity as the apparel of savages and subcultures; and looked down on the less sophisticated with an arrogance that is second to none. However, the discoveries of science were about to challenge the view that the pale complexion was a sign of superiority, and the parasol and gloves of the elegant lady were soon to be discarded.

Sunshine Healing

We have Florence Nightingale to thank for improving the health of our nation. She observed that when wounded soldiers were treated in the open air they recovered more speedily than those treated inside hospital buildings. Also, Doctor Adrian Palm in the late 19th century, proved that exposure to the sun's rays caused a definite improvement in the condition of children suffering with rickets. A few years after this, Nobel Laureate Finsen began his work in Copenhagen, experimenting with the treatment of tuberculosis by means of artificial light exposure.

Over in the Alps, stationed at an altitude of 1,450 metres, Doctor Rollier opened his Swiss clinic at Leysin (1903). Being truly sheltered from the wind, it proved to be the ideal location for the sun cure due to the clear nature of the skies. Rollier's treatment was that of measured exposure to the early morning sun, which worked on the skin and through deep penetration to the tissues below. This progressive treatment improved the terrible condition of his patients and in many cases he affected a complete cure. The patients he admitted were suffering from surgical tuberculosis and many had open sores and were emaciated and lethargic. He did not believe in over-exposing the skin to the sun at the height of the day, but rather found that the greatest benefit could be derived from moderate regular exposure in the cooler hours. He followed the example set by the animal kingdom, finding that they all seek the shade during the midday sun. In his own words: *'Cold is an enemy of the semi-starved, it is the stimulating friend of the well-fed.'* Many of his patients enjoyed skating and skiing in the sun wearing only cotton drawers. It was found that lighter coloured clothing permitted the sun's healthful rays to permeate through to the skin, whereas darker colours prevented the treatment of rickets and tuberculosis from succeeding. Rollier encouraged his patients, once their skin had turned brown, to spend as much time out in the sun as possible. He arranged for schools in the sun where children, from four to twelve years of age wearing only their loincloth, linen hat and shoes, enjoyed the benefits of the sun cure, whilst receiving an education. The treatment was slow but extremely effective. The general health of these patients was remarkable. Visitors often commented on the lack of coughs and colds among children who were so exposed. Rollier did, however, warn of the dangers of overexposure to the sun, pointing to the leathery skin of sailors as an example of the outcome.

Doctors around the world started to adopt Rollier's methods, but here in England, hospitals often managed to misapply the cure and do more harm than good. Some hospitals allowed children out of doors, but quickly put them into the shade as soon as the sun shone. Others exposed the pale white skin of ailing patients to the full force of the sun without discretion, thereby adding the agony of sunburn and sunstroke to their suffering. They failed to heed Rollier's adage: *'Fear the heat and love the light, keep your children cool and bright.'* [87] The idea soon emerged here in England that the sun was a dangerous tool. Because of this the British came to favour the 'air bath', wherein children were encouraged to play or sleep out of doors, but usually fully clothed. Needless to say, we

---

[87] Rollier: *Heliotherapy,* Oxford Medical Publications 1923.

did not experience the same success as those around the world who copied Rollier's methods without feeling the need to modify them. There is no doubt that the powerful bactericide that the sun provides, proved to be a real godsend to those fortunate enough to be exposed to it. Patients found that the sun stimulated the whole human metabolism, and improved their general health immeasurably.

During the Industrial Revolution, Britain's cities had been very dark places indeed. Houses were built so close together that the sun's rays rarely met the skin of those living in the neighbourhood. Added to this, the thick smoke that spewed out of the huge factory chimneys obliterated the sun from view. The Public Health Act of 1875 prohibited black smoke, but prosecutions were rare. Since the Act related solely to black smoke, the defendant had only to find someone willing to stand up in court and say that he saw a tinge of grey or brown in the smoke for the prosecution to collapse. The 'silver lining' of the coal strike of 1921 was the people's astonishment at seeing the beauty of their cities. Following this, efforts were made to clean up the atmosphere and great improvements in the nation's health soon followed.[88] Even so, due to England's lack of sunshine, treatment could be spasmodic, yet hospitals found the solution with the introduction of sun lamps.

Full Exposure

The modern naturist movement began in Germany following the First World War and it soon spread to France, Italy and other European countries. It took root, although hesitantly, in America as well as being adopted here in England, albeit with extreme caution. Having read the previous two chapters, you will realise that here in England it was felt necessary to take measures to cover up the nakedness of swimmers, not to mention sunbathers. So the English were not at all receptive to these new ideas. Hence the 'Simple Life Movement' or 'Back to Nature' groups were met with suspicion and opposition.

The practice of Frei-körper-kultur (an early form of German naturism), rose to popularity in Germany between the 1920s and 30s. People would gather, sharing an interest in healthier living, which would include exposing all of their skin to the sun. Cult members did not believe in polluting the body by smoking or by drinking, but stressed healthy eating habits instead. Some progressed to exposing their naked bodies to harsher weathers and recommended it. In 1924 Hans Suren published his book: *Man and Sunlight*, which was an instant success, being reprinted sixty-one times in the first year, mainly because of its

---

[88] Saleeby: *Sunlight and Health* 1923.

semi-nude photographs. By 1930, around three million Germans had embraced the naturist life style. The working class had found a new freedom, but it was short-lived. 1933 saw Hitler bring group nakedness to an end for the duration of his regime.

The very hot summer of 1928 brought changes to the dress code even in Britain. The sultry weather resulted in shorter bathing dresses with cutouts at the back, allowing ladies to obtain more of a tan.[89] It was now fashionable to have a good suntan and for it to cover as much of the body as possible. Just two years later in June 1930, nude sunbathers gathered at the Welsh Harp Reservoir, Hendon, London. They tried to hurry along the public's acceptance of total nudity, triggering a riot in the process. Locals opposing their ideology formed a mob, attacked the sunbathers and attracted the negative attention of the police and the press. Nude sunbathing was a change too far, too soon for the British public. The rapid change from coveralls to complete nudity sparked a whiplash of condemnation. Naturists, on the other hand, yearned to enjoy their newfound freedom and so they hid themselves away from public view, in the hope that tolerance would ultimately see them come out of hiding. The public, though, were sure that such deviant conduct could bring no good. General opinion was crystallising and so attention turned towards those children that still bathed naked in the river. Their nudity became objectionable and they were chased away.

For the early pioneers of naturism in Britain, sunbathing was just a part of their lifestyle choice. Copying the German example, these Gymnosophists believed in healthy eating (many were vegetarians) and physical exercise. Most practised gymnastics and swimming as part of their fitness regime. Group nakedness proved to be a great leveller bringing a new honesty and freedom to the movement's followers. Naturists began to form themselves into societies and clubs that were organised with strict rules regarding the conduct of members so as to avoid any charges of immorality. Even so, most kept their activities a secret fearing the social risk of discovery.

The naturist camps were not ideal locations; many were muddy and had few facilities. Members attended either as family groups or as individuals, but the British weather proved to be typically disappointing. After the initial surge of enthusiasm, membership declined, as many became bored with the monotony of sitting around waiting for the sun to shine. Some had gone looking for erotic adventures, but they soon found that nudity did not hold the attraction they thought it might.

Postcards featuring sexual humour had a field day with the nudist concept. These cards were popular at all seaside resorts and helped to affirm the

---

[89] Cunnington & Mansfield: *English Costume for Sports and Outdoor Recreation* 1969.

opinion of the public at large. The press put forth its view that nudism was cranky and immoral, claiming that sexual crimes were increasing on account of the nudist cult. The view that children should be brought up not to take an unhealthy interest in their bodies went to raise further suspicion about these activities. Ironically, this coincided with the dawn of the permissive society and sexual freedom. The British could not understand naturism and so naturally they shunned it.

Not in Front of the Children

Very few studies have been conducted into the effect of naturism on children, but those that are available show that youngsters brought up in such an open environment feel more positive about themselves and more comfortable with sexuality. This can prove challenging for parents who wish to bring up their children within a moral framework. Adjustment is noticeably better in cultures that lack the prudishness that we British have developed, yet children brought up in a naturist setting face unique dangers that far outweigh the benefits.

Naturist magazines featured photographs of children throughout the 60s and 70s, but their circulation much exceeded the number of naturists in the country. In fact, many naturists distanced themselves from such dubious publications. Changes in the law regarding the depiction of child nudity may have contributed to a drop in demand for such commercial magazines and their publication has since been much curtailed. Many sun clubs have these days banned all photography in order to protect the innocent. Just how such clubs can hope to completely protect children from exploiters (who would like nothing more than to experience real-life child nudity to their own gratification) is hard to imagine. This having been said, what can be seen at such clubs and beaches is nothing compared to the licentiousness available to paedophiles on the Internet. Boys and girls are displayed as though they were sexual objects; this encourages perverted reasoning and endangers the security of all children. In reality, the scandals we hear about in the news centre on children's homes, schools and sports clubs, as opposed to naturist activities. Paedophiles want to do more than just look at children and so they infiltrate organisations and befriend families, hoping to gain access to their prey. Even so, naturist organisations around the world welcome newcomers and the attraction for paedophiles proves irresistible. The fact that children are encouraged to enjoy their freedom whilst relaxing among strangers can bring them face to face with some of the most dangerous individuals they could hope to meet. It is disturbing to note that in the past, the few abusers who were brought to justice were usually allowed access to clothing catalogues in prison at which they gazed admiringly.[90] Their fascination with children evidently shows no remorse! Realisation of this fact has brought changes to the clothing catalogue. Fewer children are photographed to advertise underwear and swimwear so as to reduce the attraction of such to paedophiles. Photography has been restricted at swimming pools and a feeling of unease has now even spread to those wishing to photograph their own children holidaying on the beach.

Fears for the safety of youngsters now that paedophilia has become a household word, along with the increased volume of traffic dominating the streets, (formally the playground of the young), cause most parents to restrict the freedom of their children. But the tendency to over-react is damaging the quality of life for many youngsters. Childhood has been transformed from a time of adventure and exploration outdoors, to an indoor world of computer games, internet and television. Formally a child's mind was broadened by his experiences in the real world, whereas today his body broadens to obesity as he is held in virtual house arrest, imprisoned by fear and paranoia. Yet when it comes to moral integrity, our children may face greater dangers from their associates - other children - than they do from adults, even at home. As parents we guard our youngsters from strangers, whilst leaving the door wide open to abuse due to uncertainty as to what is morally right and appropriate between children.[91]

Regarding naturists; they have made attempts to improve the public's perception of their activities and to reassure outsiders that their conduct was only natural. For example, back in 1959 the late Edward Craven-Walker[92] produced his film: *Travelling Light*. The naturist lifestyle was depicted as an idyllic existence, but its being shown along with X-rated films[93] did little to quell the concerns of the British. In fact, the public's perception of naturism being linked with sexuality was strengthened further. The film did include pioneering underwater sequences and was the first publicly released naturist film in the

---

[90] Tate: *Child Pornography; an investigation*.

[91] It is alleged that as many as 60% of girls and 45% of boys in the UK may experience some form of sexual abuse. However, a survey involving 3,000 children carried out by the NSPCC found that youngsters are more likely to be abused by other children than by adults; attacks by strangers being very rare indeed. Regarding molestation by adults, most occurs through association with sports and community activities along with private music lessons. Even so, incest accounts for the vast majority of such abuse; meaning that for many children they are safer on the streets than they are at home!

[92] Inventor of the lava lamp and champion of English naturism.

[93] Films at this time were shown as double bills; Edward Craven-Walker had no control over the B movie shown along with his feature presentation.

Hung Out to Dry

UK.[94] Further films on the naturist theme followed, unfortunately becoming a vehicle for soft porn presentations thereafter; and reference to such even found its way into the 'Carry On' film series, with *Carry on Camping* (1968) adding again to the sexual overtones.

Later in the century a few naturist beaches were established around the coast, but fears that they had become a meeting place for gay men caused many to keep away and publicity surrounding this went on to add to the mistrust of the movement. Later still, awareness that paedophiles might visit prevented many families from attending and this has poisoned the concept of a return to Eden and replaced it with something more sinister.

A good example of the current situation is found in Dorset at the Studland Nature Reserve,[95] which hosts the largest section of naturist beach in the country, dating back to the 1930s. Studland is a very busy beach, almost as popular with water sports enthusiasts as it is with families. Naturists enjoy one-fifth of the shoreline within a recently designated boundary. Large groups of men stand to attention among the sand dunes, ready to admire and to be admired. Their statue-like figures remind one of a display of garden gnomes; ever present, but never really complementing their surroundings. Heterosexual couples make up a smaller fraction of the sunbathers, with families very much underrepresented when compared with the rest of the beach. Approximately half of those children, who are not too embarrassed to accompany their parents, feel disinclined to enter into the spirit of things. Those that do, tend to don costumes well before the onset of puberty, with most simply refusing to be seen in such a setting. The situation may be somewhat different abroad, but here in England, now that homosexuality has been established as an alternative lifestyle, gay men have come to dominate such venues. This makes families feel uncomfortable with the resultant reputation and atmosphere, one they feel powerless to

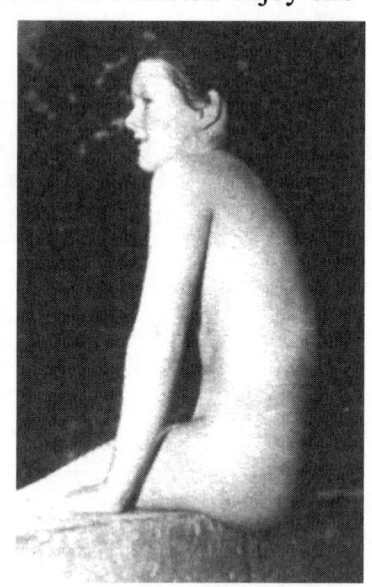

Tommy Kelly, looking quite relaxed advertising the film *Tom Sawyer* 1938. How the world has changed!

---

[94] The early Tarzan films *Tarzan of the Apes* (1918) and *Tarzan and his Mate* (1934) originally included naked scenes, but after the latter Hollywood introduced a strict anti-nudity code. Despite this, innocent skinny-dipping scenes involving children still appeared, as in *Tom Sawyer* (1938) and *Pollyanna* (1960).
[95] Owned by: The National Trust.

reform. It's not that children have changed all that much, but society has. No child wants to make a spectacle of him or herself, or to open themselves up to ridicule. Not long ago all boys may have loved to swim in the 'costume of nature', but today male nudity is associated with homosexuality, and from this boys want to distance themselves. The alternative - naturist clubs - are likewise suffering from a lack of family interest. The outlook for the movement thus sees it steering away from family orientation, into an activity reserved for exhibitionists.

In the early days sun clubs were more than just sunbathing organisations. Members used to share an interest in cultivating their bodies and in healthier living. On the whole, naturists have now departed from this notion, with most simply wanting to share in group nudity. There are still a large number of people, possibly some forty thousand, who want to live the natural life style, but British culture deems the practice shameful and deviant. On the other hand, thirteen million Germans, that's one in six, are estimated to enjoy the naturist way of life, compared to about one in a hundred Britons who can be said to have at least dabbled with it. The culture here in Britain sees nudity and immorality as inseparable and so suspicion and prejudice are unavoidable. British culture insists that people cannot be nude socially without 'hanky panky,' and many of the movement's modern devotees seem determined to prove this true. Public awareness of the vulnerability of children and the suspicions this has brought means that the final nails have now been firmly driven into the coffin of family naturism here in the UK.

The Birds and the Bees

As we have seen, a combination of concerns raised by the Industrial Revolution generated in Britain a prudishness that is quite unique. The working classes were brought right into the cities to work the machine of change. Yet the squalid unhealthy slums and the relentless overcrowding therein removed any opportunity for privacy amongst the poor. 'Coarse' people were to share the parks and beaches frequented by the 'Ladies and Gentlemen' of England, who found that they did not care for the rude uncouth nature of such lower mortals. The middle classes therefore sought to bring improvement both through regulation and education. Prudery began with the desire to preserve modesty at the seaside with the introduction of bathing machines. It continued with the separating of the sexes whilst swimming and then, once concern over the sexuality of children began to express itself, it was sustained by the desire to have even youngsters cover up on the beach. Boys were radically circumcised to moderate their indulgence in masturbation, and any interest in sexuality expressed by children was quashed by silence and secrecy. The middle classes had just about got everything in order when along came the notion that sunbathing was a good thing. More and more people began to expose their flesh to the sun, but a line had to be drawn when total nudity was suggested. Shame was seen as essential for Christians, and so the discussion of sexuality became shocking and was left for the comedian and the comic postcard to explore. But the notion that sexual interest can be removed through denial proved unworkable.

In Britain, nudity became a real taboo and so, because parents were not even explaining sexual matters to their own children, it was decided to educate them at school. Due to the prudery that had been instilled into children, the subject proved very difficult to deal with and the cultural reaction was predictable. In the late 50s the film *Merry-Go-Round* was produced to help young teenagers learn about the changes that puberty would bring. Later in 1969 the BBC produced a sex education series that similarly included footage of naked children as part of the film.[96] In both cases the producers set the children in a swimming pool situation so that viewers would feel more comfortable with the subject, but it didn't work. The BBC production caused great shock and amusement in junior school children all over the country. British children simply could not view these images without reacting with acute embarrassment and raucous laughter. Needless to say, much of the message was missed during the excitement as red faced teachers took up position in front of the TV screen in an effort to restore order and propriety. Because the British see nudity as sexual rather than natural, sex education comes under the umbrella of science rather than being taught as a part of life. Further difficulties surfaced in that teaching the science of sex was by far easier than teaching sexual morals. Children were educated out of their naivety into experimentation and promiscuity. The permissive air of the 60s and 70s turned its back on morals, and the nation has paid for this with rising divorce rates, an increase in teenage pregnancies and subsequent single parent families. The age of first sexual experience has been dropping steadily with each generation. Religion is no longer seen as being worthy of consultation since the teaching of evolution has dusted belief in God from the blackboard, and with it moral boundaries have been erased.[97] Thus we now flounder in the moral void of uncertainty. When the working classes were first drawn to the cit-

---

[96] Initially broadcast in the late evening for parental consideration and then presented to junior school children in three episodes - *Beginning, Birth, Full Circle* June $1^{st} - 15^{th}$, 1970.
[97] Evolution has become the 'new faith' replacing belief in God with scientific theories on the origin of life. Sadly this new system of credence promotes self over others (survival of the fittest); it lacks moral leadings, belittles unbelievers, and chases away any hope of Divine intervention for its adherents.

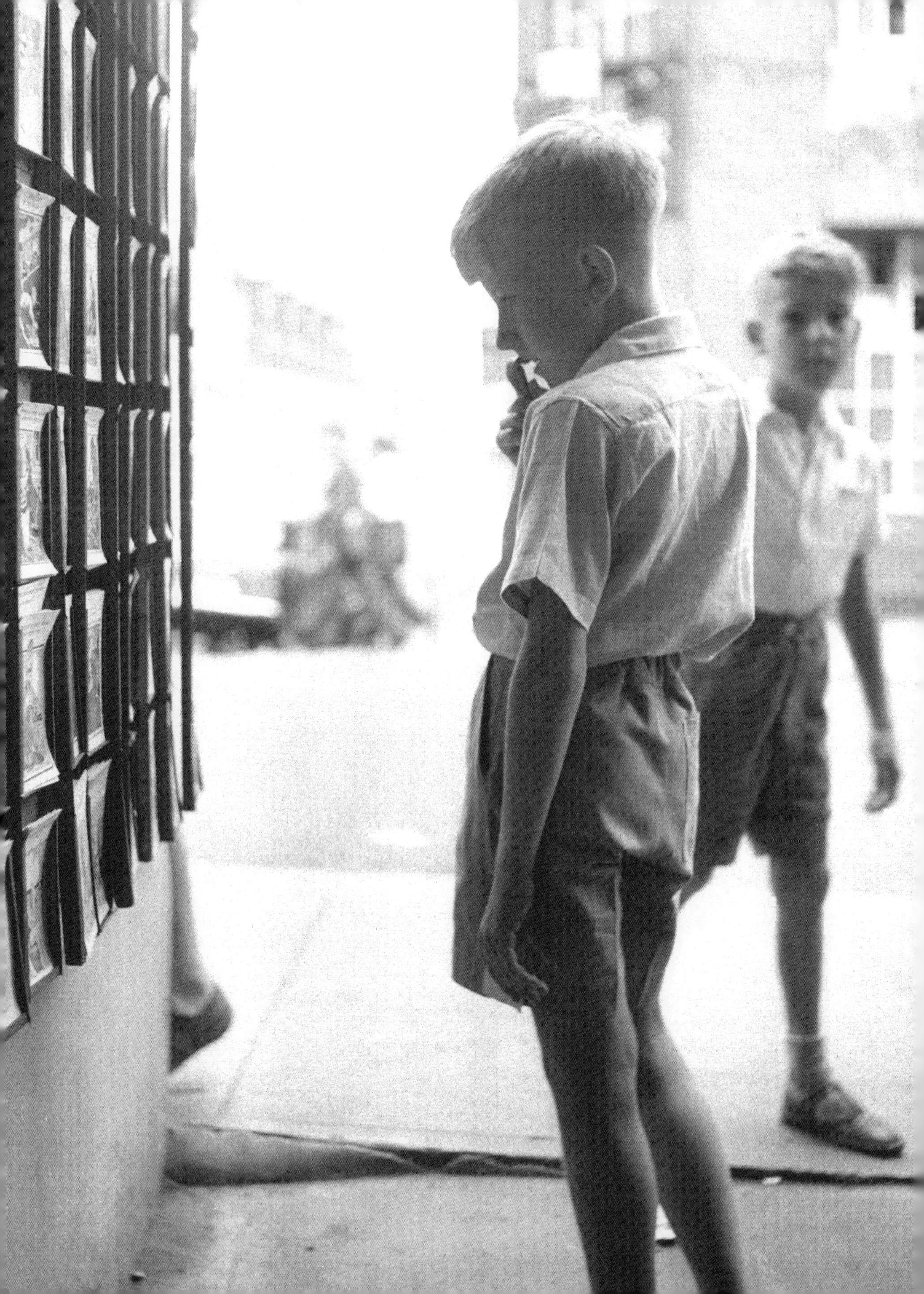

Hung Out to Dry

Previous page: The saucy postcard was a feature of all seaside resorts. It helped to galvanise the British obsession with prudery.

ies they were scolded by those of the middle class for their brazen acceptance of nudity. A complete revolution has now been achieved with naturists in Britain coming in the main from the middle class. As for the workers, they have developed an attitude that ridicules what they now see as a deviant activity.

Children have been hardest hit by the change in attitudes towards the body. Even their toys came to mirror the prudery of our nation. On the continent, baby dolls came complete with genitalia; after all, what is a baby boy without his manhood? The answer of course was a British baby boy! The British could not risk the questions that might arise from such rudeness, and so it was not until the late 1980s that toyshop owners felt comfortable stocking lifelike dolls. Needless to say, sex education was not felt essential when the existence of sex organs had for so long been denied. Such toys sent out a clear message to the children playing with them. Some missionaries ran into difficulty when befriending aboriginal children, giving them dolls to play with. Naturally the youngsters were delighted with these novel toys but after a while they removed the dolls clothing only to discover that their sex organs were missing. The children would have nothing more to do with these missionaries, reasoning that the same might happen to them. Our British culture taught children to be ashamed of themselves and to view sexual interest as wrong and ungodly. The result has been a succession of maladjusted adults that cannot come to terms with their own sexuality, let alone the education of children. As morals become less and less fashionable, children are gradually being desensitised in their relationships. Lacking the affection that once held families together, youths become sexually active very early, countless babies are aborted, children are abandoned by their natural fathers and elderly parents, once so respected, are left to fend for themselves.

Experiments with the science of sunlight forced Britons to confront their suspicions of nakedness. Our religious heritage provided the framework within which decisions had to be made regarding the rights and wrongs of sunbathing. Naturists fought their corner but failed to win the day; rather they unwittingly forced the hand of the middle classes who condemned the movement outright. Shock and embarrassment coloured the education of children in sexual matters, saucy postcards underscored and helped to reaffirm our cultural response, rounding out the prudery of British society as we know it. Yet sunbathing survived intact and the British, of all people, enjoyed seeing the transformation that a week's laying out in the sun could bring to their complexion and well-being.

What a Scorcher

With the affordability of continental holidays, Britons could travel abroad in the certain knowledge that they would return with a good suntan. By 1999, seven out of ten had enjoyed a holiday overseas. The tan came to be a symbol of status and health.[98] However, due to our unfortunate weather, we are inclined to soak up the sun whenever it shines, confident that good weather is always temporary; three sunny days and a thunderstorm being our lot in life. Holidaymakers flying to the sun took this mentality with them and serious sunburn became the reality of the working man. Even so, the suggested use of suntan lotion met with a good deal of resistance. The idea of applying costly sun cream to one's body was seen as the height of vanity by many of the working class. It was not perceived as sunburn prevention; rather the cream itself came to be viewed as a means to acquire a tan and so any one seen applying it was labelled as exceedingly vain. On the other hand camomile lotion was indispensable, being an essential holiday medicine for soothing the skin of those burnt to a crisp in the searing heat. It's not surprising therefore, that sunbathing late in the last century came under attack due to the increasing numbers of people developing skin cancer. Concerns over the thinning of the ozone layer[99] have since moved the governments of badly affected countries to protect their citizens. The 'Slip-Slop-Slap' campaign in Australia is perhaps the best-known example. The result has been a dramatic rise in the sale of sun creams and protective beachwear. The lower prices resulting from such mass marketing has led to a broader acceptance of such products, and to a lightening of the skin tone for holidaymakers. Some children now sport a skin that is so milky white that they run the risk of burning each time they venture out of doors during the summer. Their artificial way of life is mirrored by their complexion, emphasising the need for synthetic protection from the great outdoors. Parents thus need to keep up their defence regime and dutifully apply lotions each time their children venture outside, much as though they were sending their offspring into an alien environment. Moderation and balance seem some way off as the cultural swing towards a whiter skin sweeps away the benefits of natural sun exposure.

As this chapter comes to a close, you may be questioning its relevance to the social history of swimming. Yet the popularity of sunbathing became a real boon for the swimming public. As the demand for places where people

---

[98] Miriam Akhtar & Steve Humphries: *Some Liked it Hot*.

[99] Levels of chlorofluorocarbons (CFCs) have been declining in the atmosphere since the year 2000. The hole in the ozone layer over Antarctica is closing, but in 2004 it still covered 29 million square kilometres, more than three times the area of Australia. If CFC levels continue to decrease the hole could dissipate by the middle of this century.

Hung Out to Dry

would feel comfortable sunbathing in a semi-nude state rose, so lidos were built all over the country; swimming *and* sunbathing for both sexes became freely available for the first time. The association between sunshine and swimming was to be firmly implanted in the psyche of the British public and it has continued ever since. The introduction of the lido saw a move away from the early morning swim, towards a preference for bathing in warm sunny conditions. The next chapter covers the development of the lido and the exodus of swimmers from the river into purpose-built accommodation. This move, although appearing on the surface to be of great benefit to swimmers, would ultimately have dire consequences for river bathers, as we will see.

The constant feature at all lidos;
'always, everywhere, shivering boys!'
(Roger Deakin)

Chapter 5
Lidos Open, Rivers Close

Learned Swimmers

As swimming came back into vogue, people countrywide began using natural ponds, lakes and rivers for their swimming adventures. In Oxford, Parson's Pleasure[100] had been in use since the 16th century. The site still holds echoes of its past as does its companion: Dames' Delight. Parson's Pleasure officially came to its end in the mid 1990s, but cultural change started its slow death long before that. The fencing has now all gone, along with the diving board. A concrete base is all that is left of the fun, like a memorial stone on the now deserted lawns, the remains lie on the opposite bank to University Parks, Holywell. A bench in the grounds bears a plaque memorialising '…Mr H N Spalding[101] a lover of Parson's Pleasure who gave to the university the fields opposite the bathing place in order to preserve the view.' It was traditional for men and boys to bathe here in the nude. Naturally, it was screened from view on all sides and as you might expect, ladies were to either avert their eyes as they passed by in punts, or better still, to get out of the punt and walk around the fencing. C S Lewis apparently loved the place, as did many dons and undergraduates. In later times, speculation developed as to the interests of those using Parson's Pleasure and indeed, as its popularity declined, it became a magnet for suspicions. According to *Cities Of The Imagination*:[102] *'By the end, the only men who went there were those who wanted to expose themselves to passing punts and those who delighted in the company of naked young men.'*

Over the water at Dames' Delight, children from the village of New Marston regularly come to swim on sunny days, despite it's having being officially closed since 1970. You can still glimpse the concrete bases of the changing huts here, which echo the thriving popularity of this very fashionable bathing place. Built in 1934, Dames' Delight was a female and family equivalent of Parson's Pleasure, but here in later years the swimmers donned costumes rather than suspicion. Further downstream another swimming hole at St Clements adjacent to Cherwell Street lies disused and forgotten.

---

[100] A bathing place on the River Cherwell.
[101] 1877-1953.
[102] David Horan: *Oxford*.

Hung Out to Dry

Over in west Oxford, Tumbling Bay remained a thriving swimming attraction and was manned by a lifeguard until 1990. The local council have recently renovated this area' which is, I believe, one of the most easily recognisable bathing places in the country. Along with the drinking fountain, the toilets and changing cubicles have now been demolished, but back in the eighties, the place was alive with people on sunny days. They enjoyed a free swim in this man-made pool, which resembles one you might more likely expect to find indoors, both in size and design. There were originally two pools in use, the ladies swam upstream in one enormous pool and the gents swam in the lower reaches. A weir separates the two, the sound of which is heard long before this secret place comes into view; thus the name Tumbling Bay! At the turn of the century, work commenced on restoring the weir. Part of the men's pool has been cleared and swimmers enjoy using this section of the facility even today! The pool is approached through West Oxford Recreation Ground on Botley Road, and the remains can be visited by walking to the park's north-eastern corner. Long Bridges in south Oxford was yet another popular bathing place, with both men's and ladies quarters, along with bathing places at Cutteslowe, St Ebbes and Wolvercote among others, showing just how important river bathing used to be in Oxford.

Cambridge was not of course to be outdone and the Sheep's Green bathing complex is still very evident. The large rectangular paddling pool is extremely popular with local children. Adjacent to it, a footbridge crosses a tributary of the Cam and the boys' and girls' bathing places lie to the left and right respectively. Walking across the field, another bridge separates the men's and ladies' quarters. For the men a five-stage diving board reaching up some fifteen feet, a water chute and a springboard with a tremendous run up ensured the success of the attraction (pictured above). Sadly, river bathing officially came to an end here in the 1960s and interest was transferred to the open-air pool on Jesus Green.

The Big City

In London, the ponds of Hampstead Heath have always been used as swimming holes, as has the Serpentine Lake in Hyde Park. In the 1890s the Victoria Park Lake was concreted and its surroundings paved. This lake was very popular, with as many as 25,000 using it at a time, as illustrated in the introduction.[103] A lido in Victoria Park ultimately replaced the lake for swimming, but this meant a move away from the swimmers' natural surroundings. Years later when the lido eventually closed, swimming in the park sadly came to an end. This is a pattern that has been repeated all over the country; the move away from swimming in the wild, toward more civilised attractions, which has ultimately led to the near extinction of wild swimming almost everywhere. How though did this happen and why?

Swimming in the Serpentine[104] has a long history. The National Swimming Society arranged one of the first competitions held there on August 6th 1837. The prizes included an attractive silver medallion and a golden guinea for the winner, with a bronze medallion and a half guinea for the runner up. *The Pictorial Times* of 1843 reported:

> *'Nothing is more conducive to health of body and energy of mind than a cool, refreshing, invigorating bath in clear water on a summer's morning. We would have swimming made part of the projected system of national education; without this adjunct, any plan for the instruction of the rising generation would be defective.*
>
> *On Friday morning 18th August, at a very early hour, the vicinity of the Serpentine, in Hyde Park, was crowded with an immense number of persons, amounting, we should say, to twenty thousand, to view the grand swimming match, which was advised to come off on that morning...'*

When you compare the action and excitement of a football match to the comparatively tame activities of a swimming event, is it not remarkable that so many were prepared to rise so early to take pleasure in such events?

From December 1864 the Serpentine Swimming Club began to organise events; the annual Christmas morning races thus began and since 1903 the cov-

---

[103] Open from 4 – 8 a.m. in the summer months. Park regulations restricted nudity to boys under ten in 1905.
[104] Hyde Park, London.

eted Peter Pan Cup has been the prize awarded to the winner. Its value was greatly magnified by the fact that for many years it was presented by none other than Sir James Barrie himself.[105] The Peter Pan connection will strike a chord with all swimmers, but especially those adults who have not forgotten how to enjoy themselves in and around water.

The club's headquarters were beneath an old elm tree on the south side of the lake, with a wooden bench for clothing being the only facility. Fred Houghton says in *Breaking the Ice*:

> *'Indeed it can truthfully be said we were as close to nature as one could ever wish to be and how we loved it. Even the swans were given names to which they answered. There was no shelter other than that given by the trunk of a burley old elm. We were in full view of the riders in Rotten Row and this fact subsequently brought about the first change.'*

This first change saw a mound created the full length of the course to hide the bathers from view. However, the lack of screening for those getting changed led to many complaints of indecency. The tradition of early morning bathing ensured that the spectacle would not be witnessed by women, who were very well aware of the need to make themselves scarce in the early hours so as not to see what the 'stork' saw. Even so, a protest was made in the House of Commons, referring to disgusting scenes observed on the banks of the Serpentine, which were allegedly more disgusting than those to be witnessed in darkest Africa. Boys were customarily chased out of the lake because they insisted on skinny-dipping and this became the theme of many amusing photographs, as depicted on the front cover.

In the old days, a diving board was provided for these early bathers. This was really just a plank that stood on four posts in the water, with another plank connecting it to the bank. The connection was only in position for two hours, being packed away promptly at 9.00 a.m. as the boatmen (RHS) were always anxious to get home to their breakfast.

Children flocked to the Serpentine especially because they could swim there for free. Many simply could not afford to swim in the newly created indoor pools despite the relatively low admission charges; besides outdoor swimming was fun and accessible. Commander Gerald Forsberg remembers:[106]

---

[105] 1860-1937 creator of *Peter Pan*.
[106] Titmuss: *Breaking the Ice* 1964.

Lidos Open, Rivers Close

'My own initial aquatic adventure was to swim across the lake. This not only required a certain standard of high physical ability, but also an equal and opposite standard of low animal cunning, because the Royal Humane Society boat was stationed in the most strategic place for just the express purpose of stopping such dangerous young voyages. It was necessary to wait until the R.H.S boatman had his attention quite firmly diverted elsewhere – not infrequently by an accomplice-cum-decoy. When the currently devised stratagem was operating successfully, one made a mad sprint for the other side. The centre line of the lake was the point of no return. From there on, one could pretend - in best Nelsonian fashion - not to hear or see the boatman's urgent signals to return. Or one could innocently plead a most pressing necessity to land on the nearest shore for a rest. I succeeded in such enterprises some half-dozen times before being recognised as a regular transgressor and 'warned-off' formally. In quite blunt straight forward fashion too; R.H.S boatmen were frequently ex-sailors with a memorably blistering vocabulary and a muscular expertise with a well-aimed wallop.'

It was with mixed feelings that members of the Serpentine Swimming Club discovered that the government were planning to create a lido on their beloved lake. A deputation sought an interview with the commissioner of works, George Lansbury, a Poplar Labour politician. The result was very satisfactory in that he gave categorical assurances that all the privileges that the club had hitherto enjoyed would be respected and that admittance to the lido would remain free of charge for those engaged in club activities. The creation of the lido forced club members a little further from 'Mother Nature' (from 1930 costumes were insisted upon), but it did not prevent these pioneers of open-air swimming from pursuing their activities. Mr Lansbury had come to realise that being the President of the Board of Works gave him authority over the Royal Parks including the Serpentine. It was he that proposed the building of the lido, but he had great difficulty in obtaining public funds. The main idea of the lido was to provide discreet changing facilities, so that passers-by did not have to witness the bare flesh of changing swimmers - 'indecent exposure'. In order to obtain Royal Consent, Lansbury took water samples to King George V, who personally examined them through a microscope before giving his approval for construction to commence.

According to Douglas Goldring: *'So mean was the attitude of the governing class that Lansbury had to fight tooth and nail against Tory obstruction to obtain for Londoners the right to bathe in their own Serpentine, in their own park.'* Writing in *Punch*,[107] Eric Keown reports on the struggle: people would *'...write letters to the press urging the impropriety of giving London's bodies a chance to cool themselves in London's water...'* (Lansbury) *'ploughed resolutely ahead with his schemes for making life a little brighter, especially for children in the parks... He was called a sentimentalist and even worse.'*

The Times led with *'Mr Lansbury's devastations'* and reported that the parks were being endangered *'for the sake of privileged parties of individuals.'* Eric Keown continues: *'having failed on public and religious grounds the objectors now switched to the aesthetic'* (complaints over the colour of the changing marquees). There was outrage over the prospect that near nudity was to be *encouraged* in the park. Initially, swimmers charged at 3d a head were only tolerated earlier than 10.00 a.m. in the summer months. In the winter, swimmers could not bathe after the 6.30 a.m. curfew on weekdays or 9.00 a.m. on Sundays. Leo Fabian of the Serpentine Swimming Club was caught red-handed by a policeman being found swimming in the lake at *9.02 a.m.* on a Sunday morning. He was summonsed and duly fined one shilling for this grave misdemeanour.

Despite all the objections to the lido, we find that no sooner was it opened than thousands of Londoners flocked to it to enjoy its pleasures. *'Shoals of citizens and their young swam bravely to and fro, while the air rang with the cheerful sound of spring boards drumming.'*

The lido proved to be anything but the eyesore the pessimists had predicted. *'Mr Ted Stoter,*[108] *the Lido's paternal ex-Mariner Superintendent, who looks like a jovial umpire in his white coat... came to the Lido in its first week... one of the chief pleasures of the job he would exchange for none (he said) is meeting the children of his first small charges. On the question of the modern child... If you shout at him, he says, you get nowhere, but if you appeal to his humanity he is yours at once. "The other day," said Mr. Stoter, "a lad began to make a nuisance of himself. I asked him if his dad was in work? 'Yus', says the boy. 'Right,' I said, 'so am I. D'ye want me to get the sack?' 'Corse not,' says the boy. 'Well, I will if you go on creating.' And that was the end of that." '*

In the early days, people were not bothered about getting brown, *'they were too swaddled for one thing and anyway they were not supposed to hang about after they had finished swimming.'*[109] But as customs changed, so the lido filled out with bathers lying in the sun. The support of King George V certainly

---

[107] July 6th 1949. For background on East End living conditions: *The Midwife* - Jennifer Worth.
[108] Ted Stoter was made an OBE for his services to the lido. Following his death his ashes were scattered in the lido gardens, as has been the case for many members of the Serpentine Swimming Club.
[109] Quotations from *Punch* July 6th 1949.

contributed to the huge success of this magnificent lido. The original swimming area was twice its current size and it soon became a popular place for Londoners to sunbathe and picnic. Officially, mixed bathing began in 1932 and, with the benefit of the marquees, the fairer sex could change without fear of exposure. However, in the winter, the changing facilities were taken down and so the lido reverted to a mainly male sanctum for the duration of the cold season.

Over the years there have been many concerns regarding water quality. Originally, the lake was fed from street sewers and so chlorine was sprayed into the water from a boat to sanitize it. Later a chlorination plant was used to pump chemicals into the lake around the perimeter of the swimming quarter. Today, it is fed by two wells and there has been no need to chlorinate the water for some time. This is good news for swimmers, as in the past chlorine levels have proved to be a public danger. The water now is cleaner than at many indoor pools and even though it takes on a green hue, it is of drinkable quality.

I visited the lake in July 1999, the lido having reopened three years earlier. The Club still meet every day for an early morning swim, usually gathering between 6.30 and 9.30 in the morning. On Christmas day 2008, sixty-seven swimmers plunged into the water for the traditional dip. The lido is attractively presented with a paddling pool and play park for the youngsters, along with sun loungers and a large swimming area for the rest. Sadly, with all the improvements, diving is strictly prohibited and so one's adventures are somewhat stifled.

Charges for using the lido were reasonable, but children under fifteen were not admitted without an adult. Whilst I was there, it became apparent that some local youngsters preferred to swim without trying to pay their dues and thus risking rebuff. It's very easy for them to get in, as the security gates are only about three foot high and remain unlocked. Topless sunbathing is allowed in the beach area and one young lady had taken advantage of this. The visiting youngsters were quick to notice the attraction and were very vocal in their admiration. This group went on to enjoy the lake for some time, before being chased away by the Park Ranger who brought the excitement to an end. This scene put me in mind of the many photographs (such as the one on the front cover), that caused Lansbury to open up the lake in the first place. With all the improvements at the lido we see that history has gone full circle. In the old days, boys were chased out of the lake because they insisted on skinny-dipping (for many, there was no option as they had no undergarments to wear and they certainly could not afford swimwear). Today the chase goes on, but the reason is even clearer; unaccompanied children are simply not welcome. The British idea that children should be seen and not heard is especially evident in the swimming situation. We do not tolerate children for very long. When we see

Hung Out to Dry

them gathered together, we tend to assume that they are up to no good and insist that they move away.

The Lido

What, then, accounted for the popularity of the lido throughout the nation? Well, it would seem that by the end of the 19th century, great progress was being made in the provision of libraries and bathhouses countrywide. But following the First World War it was realised that improvements still needed to be made to occupy the leisure time of the masses. Public parks provided wonderful amenities for townsfolk; most provided a paddling pool along with swings and slides for the children. The construction of open-air pools and lidos grew out of the government's concern for the health of the nation, combined with a desire to meet the need for leisure activities. During the First World War, 40% of those recruits who received a medical examination were placed in the lowest possible category for health: 'C'. They were found unfit for service abroad, lacking both height and strength. The physical weakness of so many prospective soldiers sent a shudder through the nation, and it dawned on the authorities that something needed to be done about the general health of the population. Medical theories about the benefits of sunlight and fresh air created new attitudes throughout the country. The war itself had had a telling effect upon the nation's health. Food shortages and a reduction in the amount of animal fat available for consumption (due to its being used in the production of high explosives during the First World War), contributed to a rise in rickets and tuberculosis.[110] Sunlight was seen as both a preventative and a cure. In the late 1920s and early 1930s, countries in Europe and America set a trend by providing outstanding facilities for their people. The lido (from the Latin litus, meaning shore) was just what the nation needed. It provided open-air swimming along with much needed sunbathing terraces. Swimming competitions were regularly held and most lidos provided ample room for spectators.

Peterborough Lido is an excellent example, with room for hundreds to watch swimming competitions from its first floor balcony, which is built around the perimeter of the pool. This pool is also a good example in that it includes a large grassy area for sunbathing and picnicking; a play park for the children; a paddling pool and shallow training pool, along with the large main pool. Further attractions used to include a water chute and a terrace of diving boards. Cafés added an air of sophistication to the visit and there was something for everyone. These lidos were designed to fulfil the need for holiday recreation. When

---

[110] According to: *Farewell my Lido*; a Thirties Society Production.

looking at photographs featuring such lidos in their heyday, the success of the venture is immediately apparent. Due to health and safety regulations this pool, which opened in 1936, has had its maximum capacity more than halved from an original three thousand swimmers. The diving tower was dismantled in the 1980s, but an inflatable water chute, somewhat like those used to escape from an aircraft, replaced it; this has now gone as well because of new regulations. The children's water-chute has been vandalised and money is not forthcoming to repair it. Despite all the changes, Peterborough Lido is still quite popular, especially on sunny days. In 1995 during a period of sunshine lasting five weeks, the lido made a huge profit; the pool was filled to capacity daily by 10.00 a.m. and the doors had to be closed! The lido is still owned by the council (it is a listed building), but it is now run, as are many others, by a private company as part of a package along with other leisure complexes in the city. Any losses are thus subsidised by profits from the rest of the group.

Sadly, all outdoor pools come in for more than their fair share of vandalism. On a summer's evening as many as a hundred illicit swimmers will break into the pool. The consequence of this is that a pool cover cannot be used to retain water temperature at night; for fear that trespassers might drown under it. Paying guests thus suffer cooler waters, in order that the lives of illegal users are not put at risk. Greater security is an option, but as there is no money to repair the water chute, the building of a higher wall is unlikely.

Times Change

With the advent of Health and Safety Regulations, lidos have lost much of their appeal. Diving boards have been removed from nearly all swimming baths and water slides at outdoor pools are quite rare these days. In the years up to the end of the 1930s, many pools were unsupervised. People used to look after each other, those being the days of community responsibility and self-reliance. Nowadays children grow up thinking that there will always be someone ready to rescue them if they get into difficulties. They take this idea with them to the seaside and view the beach environment much as a giant wave pool, taking risks that show a complete lack of respect for the ocean.

Most lidos used to contain unheated water. This was seen as a real benefit in the past, but with changes in social conditions and improvements in household heating, the nation has become used to higher temperatures and only lidos with heated water now prove to be popular on cooler days. However, when the sun shines it's a completely different story, as we have seen. Lidos become so busy that they often have to shut their doors in the early afternoon because they cannot safely admit any more people.

Hung Out to Dry

Many town councils have seen the dereliction of their lidos. Their lack of support for most of the year is a major reason given for allowing them to fall out of use, but this proves to be a real loss of amenity for the residents of these towns. It should be remembered that most *indoor* swimming pools make little or no profit. It only takes two or three weeks of good weather to take an outdoor pool out of deficit but, sadly, many councillors actively discourage the maximisation of these facilities. In Hayle, Cornwall, the lido attracts many local people and particularly children during the holidays. This is especially remarkable when you consider how close it is to one of the best beaches in the country and the fact that the water is unheated. The springboard has had to go of course, and the pool has turned into something of a childminding service during the school holidays. I was told by one of the lifeguards that in recent times, permission to display a new sign on the roadside alerting passers-by to the existence of the pool was denied. This, it was hoped, would have drawn people in and raised profits. Sadly, it was decided to leave the peeling old wooden sign that simply read 'Swimming Pool' in place, thus preventing it from becoming too popular. However in 2001, Hayle council relented and a new sign now appears on the roadside. The residents and holidaymakers of Hayle are fortunate as most councils would like to see an end to their lido and many have already seen their wish come true or are working towards it.

Moving up country, the lido at Weston-Super-Mare had such an attractive arched diving stage that the Department of the Environment listed it because of its outstanding interest and design. The unique seven platform concrete structure was a credit to the nation. Sadly, the stage was quickly de-listed before the council granted itself permission to demolish it in February 1982, thus ensuring that the pool could never be resurrected.

From Good to Bad

Paddling pools require a degree of attention each week during the summer and because of this many have been turned into sandpits or else lie empty. The idea that sunlight and fresh air add to a child's health has now been diluted with warnings of the danger of sunburn and the gazing eyes of paedophiles. But, the most significant reason centres, I feel, on the desire for a reduction in expenses and all other reasons pale next to this.

The net result of the move away from providing these public amenities has been a steady increase in juvenile crime. This has led to a feeling on the part of disenchanted teenagers that people do not understand their needs and that society does not care about them. Those affected most by the closure of lidos and paddling pools, are the group most in need of them, young males.

Lidos Open, Rivers Close

*Unequalled elsewhere in Britain;
the diving stage at Weston-Super-Mare.*

Over the years of the 20th century, great improvements in sanitation significantly improved the health of the nation. Where poor sanitation does exist though, children gain lifelong immunity from diseases such as polio by becoming infected at a young age. As hygiene improved, children were robbed of this natural immunity, making them susceptible in later life. Although most children showed no symptoms, in others, paralysis was the result and for some this meant spending the rest of their lives in an iron lung. Between the years 1920-1960 there were many polio epidemics, until artificial immunity was made available via vaccination. Belief that the disease was transmitted through water closed the lidos during such epidemics. Rivers became out of bounds to swimmers through fears of contracting polio and the feeling that river water is unsuitable for swimming remains to this day.

More Harm than Good

By the end of the 20th century, clinical standards of living were seen to be harming the health of children. Youngsters were developing allergic reactions such as asthma, because their bodies could find nothing to fight off in the way of dirt and germs, which until recent times was the expected result of living in the natural world. The protective immune system of privileged children in the West thus turned on the body itself. From babyhood, humans naturally ingest a good quantity of dirt. By protecting children in an unnaturally clean environment, we have unwittingly done them more harm than good (asthma, diabetes and cancer are all conditions to which one may be sensitised due to this move away from exposure to the natural environment). It is therefore not surprising that many less fortunate children, the ones allowed out in all weathers and who run home with a little dirt on them, seem to be so healthy. Children who bathe regularly in rivers do so without ill effects, whilst those from germ-free households fall prey to every unfamiliar infection. In contrast though, clinical conditions are lacking in many UK hospitals, which means that a good 10% of deaths in hospital are said to be the result of infections caught whilst in residence. Nowadays hospitals lack the distinctive smell of phenolic disinfectant and outside contractors offering the lowest prices are entrusted with much of the cleaning. This means that your entering hospital puts you at a much greater risk of dying of a deadly infection than your entering much of Britain's open water!

Of course you are not likely to drown in hospital and it's alarming to discover that three times as many people drown in the country's inland waters than those lost at the coast. What is more shocking is that of the two hundred and forty-eight souls drowned in rivers and streams in 1999, only ten were swimming related![111] Strong currents washed three away, two resulted from diving accidents, three simply got into difficulties with the cause of the other two deaths being unknown. In total there were five hundred and sixty-nine people drowned during the year; forty-five of these deaths were related to swimming. This was unusually high and was possibly due to the hot weather. How did so many drown? Although swimming is shunned whenever drowning occurs, the most dangerous activities would appear to be walking, fishing and boating. For example, no-one drowned whilst swimming in the canal, but forty-three others who had been simply walking, playing or working nearby did. Perhaps signs reading: 'No swimming', should be replaced with: 'Walkers take care.' This statistic is especially interesting in view of the fact that so many young people swim in locks, slide down weirs and jump from bridges. How can this continue to be so without a string of fatalities? Sadly, fourteen people died in swimming pools, including the only drowning in Leicester; another fourteen drowned in their vehicles following mishaps; and a further thirty-one at home in the bath. Wherever water is to be found, the danger of drowning is ever present. But when we compare the press reports of five thousand deaths related to infections caught in hospital each year and the comparatively low number of deaths

---

[111] Older statistics used, as opposed to the latest figures, out of respect for those affected.

from swimming incidents, as opposed to walking, etc, surely it is unreasonable to prohibit swimming on these grounds?

No one wants to see a life tragically snuffed out. The most obvious answer is to provide lifeguards, as is the case at Hampstead Heath in London. In reality though, this is not always practical, especially if councils do not want to encourage swimming. Therefore, swimmers themselves need to take precautions. Children who lack ability should not swim without some form of adult supervision. It is unwise to swim alone even if you are a good swimmer and whenever swimming, you must stay alert to the dangers.

One aspect that cannot be overlooked is the role that *alcohol* plays in drownings each year. It would seem that drinking causes one to overestimate personal abilities, whilst at the same time reducing actual performance. This combination often proves deadly; so we are well advised not only to avoid drinking and driving, but also diving, swimming, walking and biking by water.[112]

It has to be said that the safest place to swim remains the indoor pool, but many children find the stifling atmosphere an unattractive alternative to the joys of the river, lake or canal. Many children will swim several times during a sunny day if given the opportunity; this of course is not practical for most, as indoor pools run on a session basis and the activity proves very expensive.[113] A good alternative is the outdoor pool or lido. Usually these pools admit swimmers on an all-day basis and they throng with children during good weather. Sadly, the vast majority of these pools have now been closed and so the only real alternative is the river, lake or canal.

Many of us take holidays in the sun and enjoy continental swimming pools, where we have less chance of finding a lifeguard than a stick of Blackpool rock. The reason we find this acceptable reveals something about our cultural heritage. Drownings do of course occur; but in Britain we insist on doing 'the right thing', whereas when we leave the country, we become more relaxed and less rigid. We return to watching out for our own children and those of others, just as people used to before the days when we expected everything done for us. On many beaches in England, holidaymakers swim in the sea, with no guardian to rescue them; sometimes people drown,[114] but the beach is not closed because of this, rather a reminder is given that care must be taken.

---

[112] RoSPA: *Drowning Statistics in the UK* 1999-2000.

[113] In 2009 a government health initiative saw the over-sixties and under 16's swimming for free country wide; a scheme which was to be extended to all ages ready for the 2012 London Olympics. Sadly the financial crisis saw all the funding removed in the summer of 2010.

[114] Despite conditions or dangers, swimmers at the seaside are rarely discouraged, thus protecting the profits of the tourist trade.

Hung Out to Dry

Should the same not apply to our rivers and lakes? British education in water safety is about as good as our sex education used to be: 'if you're not going to do it, you don't really need to know about it.' Would it not be better to educate people about *where* it is safer to swim? The signs that prohibit swimming, simply add to the problem by pushing swimmers out of sight and into danger.[115]

Another disturbing statistic shows that although many of those who drowned had learned to swim, their abilities did not save them. Many see this as proof of the dangers of open water swimming. Yet it is possible to drown even whilst under the watchful care of lifeguards at public swimming pools, as did seven during 1999. Is it really surprising, that those whose experience of swimming is restricted to warm water pools and then only in appropriate dress, find themselves in difficulty when they end up in cold water unexpectedly? Many find that the shock of the cold inhibits rational thought and they flounder. Others find that they simply cannot stay afloat, let alone swim, when fully clothed. A lack of knowledge results in many a desperate struggle against river flows, which could safely be avoided if experience has been gained beforehand. Our expectations for schoolchildren are so low that the swimming skills they master prove far from satisfactory.

Save the Children

Surely all of this argues for a wider experience of open water swimming, as this is the real lifesaver, not pool training indoors. This lesson has been learned in Fowey, Cornwall. Each year in June, the village school at Polruan organises a swim across the harbour for the ten and eleven year olds. The event is much encouraged, as many locals have drowned here, trying to cross the river having missed the last ferry. The swimmers train both in a swimming pool and in the harbour and this common sense approach provides both the experience and training needed to view the dangers objectively. Parents and children take the matter very seriously, as their senior school education involves a twice-daily ferry crossing. For the children, the sense of accomplishment is obvious; 95% of them can swim a mile by the time they leave.

The history of Eton contains a similar lesson. In the early days, there was a superstition at the school that a youngster drowned there every three

---

[115] *BMJ* reports that drowning is the second most frequent cause of death in 26 of the world's richest countries among children up to 14 years of age. 'Infants are most likely to drown in the home (usually in the bathtub); toddlers in bodies of water close to the home such as swimming pools or ponds; and older children in natural bodies of water such as lakes and rivers.' Experts recommend that children should not be allowed to swim alone or in isolated areas.

years. In 1839, a boy named Montague was lost after being dragged out of his boat by a barge rope. It was decided that in future boys would have to be able to swim before they would be allowed boating privileges. There were four swimming places constructed on the river, with Cuckoo Weir being made available for the younger boys. The 'non Nants', as non-swimmers were known, had to prove their ability by swimming 250 yards, treading water and swimming on their backs. The 'pass', as it was called, resulted in about two hundred boys qualifying each year. The fact that there was no swimming pool constructed until 1956 (outdoor) meant that all the training was done in open water. Etonian boys would thus experience swimming in the very environment in which they would find themselves, should misfortune strike them. During the next one hundred and sixteen years there was only one drowning incident and it would appear that no amount of preparation could have averted it.[116] This fine record shows a possible benefit in open water swimming over that of training at indoor pools, especially when it comes to self-preservation. (The river is now used only for boating; it is rumoured that the pool was built to replace river bathing due to polio fears).

I do not suggest that schools abandon the indoor pool and begin training their pupils in open water; but there is an important lesson that we miss at our peril. Those who learn to swim in the shielding environment of the indoor heated pool gain a false sense of security as swimmers. It is always easy to get out of such a pool with its steps, ladders and low sides. Swimming in this setting does little to prepare one for misadventure. Accidents usually mean a sudden and unexpected entry into *cold* water, often with a current and possibly no obvious means of getting out. Add to this one's being hampered by shoes and clothing and it's not hard to see how many such mishaps end in tragedy. The real world environment comes as such a shock that panic often inhibits rational thinking. Tragically, statistics reveal that the vast majority of those who drowned were far from being capable swimmers. However things need not remain this way. Swimmers have become institutionalised at the public baths so it is no wonder that they find it hard to fend for themselves in the real world. Open water swimming on the other hand has an inoculationary effect in that it furnishes firsthand experience of: 1) the crucial need to check water depth before diving or jumping in; 2) the difficulties in getting out of a flowing river; 3) currents and how to navigate them and 4) when the weather is especially cold, the experienced river swimmer will know just why to take extra care when walking near water. To prevent people swimming in open water deprives them of these benefits and might even do them more harm than good. It seems ironic

---

[116] Frank Sachs: *The Complete Swimmer*.

Hung Out to Dry

that outdoor swimming was once *encouraged* as a measure to reduce the number of drownings nationwide, whereas nowadays such swimming is *discouraged* for the very same reasons.

Children delight in swimming in the warmth of the indoor pool, but for their skill to be life-preserving there is no substitute for real life open water experience.

Dirty Rivers

All kinds of maladies are supposed to result from river bathing. The most publicised threat is Weil's disease.[117] A comprehensive report headed *'Health Hazards Associated with the Recreational Use of Water'*,[118] indicated that the benefits we get from using water for fun far outweigh the risks. Dr Robin Philip, an epidemiologist at the University of Bristol, stands as a voice of reason amid the

---

[117] Ironically in Australia, signs warn swimmers that they share their waters with sharks and crocodiles; here in Britain river bathing is often denied supposedly to protect swimmers from microscopic bugs.

[118] South Western Regional Health Authority: *Report of a working party*. Bristol, December 1991.

morass of media paranoia. By studying the history of the disease, he has been able to assess the risks to water users, including swimmers, stating:

> *There are on average each year in the UK, some 2.5 cases of Weil's disease associated with bathing and water sports (i.e. one case among every two million annual recreational users). As the case fatality rate in the UK is 10-15 per cent, the chances of dying from Weil's disease associated with bathing and water sports is about 1:20 million exposed persons (i.e. one case in the UK every four years).*[119]

Swimmers should remember though, that it is not impossible to contract Weil's disease; risk is apparently heightened if a swimmer has an open cut, especially to the head. If you experience 'flu like symptoms within two to nineteen days of swimming in open water you should inform your doctor, so that he can make an informed diagnosis.[120] It should not be overlooked that anglers are equally at risk! The fact that they rarely enter the water in no way offers protection from the disease. Interestingly, most fishermen have to pay for a licence before they can practise their sport and yet authorities are in no way perturbed as they not only allow but very much encourage fishing activities. It's a shame that the same liberality afforded to anglers is not also shown towards swimmers. Instead they suffer persecution rather than encouragement, purely because of the bad press related to Weil's disease, with outrageous claims having been made regarding the risks to which swimmers are exposed. There is of course a slight chance that swimmers will encounter this problem. Nonetheless, by comparison, your chances of dying in a road accident are one in nine thousand six hundred[121] in any one year; so the emphasis on the risks of Weil's disease at one in twenty million are, I think you will agree, very much overstated.[122]

Unlike swimming pools, rivers are natural environments and support all kinds of wildlife; swimmers therefore need to be aware of the danger of becoming entangled in weeds. What often happens in such a case is that the swimmer thrashes violently with his legs in the hope of freeing himself, only to find that

---

[119] Environmental Health, October 1992 page 295: This report covers all cases of the disease between 1982 and 1991, concluding that: 'the risks of contracting the disease and of dying from it, therefore seem to be lower among recreational water sports enthusiasts than for the general population.'

[120] Source: BCU advice regarding Weil's disease.

[121] Dr Robin Philip: *Environmental Health*, October 1992 page 295.

[122] The British Canoeing Union set out to assess the risks water sports enthusiasts are exposing themselves to when it comes to Weil's disease. They put the chances of catching and actually dying from the disease for a canoeist at 1:333,000 (*Environmental Health* October 1992 page 295).

he becomes even more firmly entangled. It cannot be over stressed that swimming should take place in areas free of weeds. Council authorities could easily arrange for a stretch of river to be cleared of this danger and so eliminate the risk of entanglement. If you ever find yourself in this predicament, the best advice might be to keep afloat by using your arms only and gradually wriggle your way free as you swim with the current, but on no account should you struggle.

Another risk arises from the practice on the part of the Environment Agency to allow water authorities to pollute our waterways with sewage effluent,[123] although, of course, it is the government that sets the standards that the agency goes on to enforce. You have to be balanced in the stand you take on this, because similar pollution occurs in bathing waters all around the British coast.[124] Levels of bacteriological pollution vary with water flow and the action of sunlight in cleaning it up. The best, and in many cases, only guide to water quality available inland, is experience. If local children swim regularly at a certain spot without harm, the worst you might expect is a mild tummy upset following your swim. For those keen on trying a dip on the wild side, a drink of cola following your adventures can help ward off many undesirables.

To put things into balance, let us look again at the one in ten deaths that are said to occur in hospital as the result of an infection caught whilst staying there. The chances of a child contracting a deadly disease when entering a hospital are much higher than those he encounters on entering open water. Of course, things could be better on both counts, but the desire to improve conditions in hospitals will, I'm sure, bring about swifter changes than any number of protests about water pollution.

If waterways were as polluted as many insist, would it not be better to fence them off so as to protect ill-fated walkers? The fact is that this has been tried already, as happened for example in 1952 when part of the Rochdale canal was closed down and became Manchester's unofficial dumping ground.[125] This particular stretch of water runs through the densely populated Miles Platting district. Barbed wire fences were put up to keep people out, but even so there was a child drowned there nearly every year. The fences ensured that there was

---

[123] Hepatitis 'A' is a viral infection with an incubation period of two to six weeks. The onset of the illness is abrupt, with symptoms including loss of appetite, fever, nausea and abdominal discomfort, to be followed in a few days by jaundice. Although the risk of contracting this disease is slight, if you become ill with these symptoms your doctor should be informed of your aquatic activities.
[124] In 2002 95% of UK beaches complied with the European Bathing Water Directive 2001 according to Michael Meacher, the Environment Minister.
[125] Colin Ward: *The Child in the City* 1978.

never any one around to rescue these hapless explorers. In the end, it was decided to remove the fencing and reduce the depth of the canal to no more than seven inches. The design meant that water cascaded over the lock gates. This proved a great attraction to children, who loved to bathe in the resultant waterfalls and who came to view the transformed canal as a giant paddling pool.[126] Fencing rivers off is surely undesirable, as this example testifies.

Many rivers have been lost to swimmers due to pollution, the Thames being a prime example. At one time, barge loads of sand were regularly dumped on its banks to make beaches for Londoners to enjoy. London-on-Sea, as it was affectionately known, attracted crowds of would-be holidaymakers to the waterfront of the big city. Its popularity can instantly be seen from photographs of such river beaches and of divers making the most of the embankment. Sadly, these opportunities have now been removed. Although initially pollution was to blame for this, why is it that with an improvement in water quality, swimmers have not returned to the Thames in the same way as the salmon have? Could it be that nowadays negative attitudes toward river bathing are the real cause of prejudice against the swimmer? Over the last fifty years we have seen such a change in attitudes that Britain is hardly recognisable as the nation of swimmers it used to be. Today, instead of encouraging river swimming, most people feel that the activity is unwise, if not intrinsically wrong, even verging on the criminal. Salmon may have returned to the Thames, but the swimmers' return is not dependant on water quality, rather it is public opinion and prejudice that prevents their reintroduction to its waters.

Undercover

Despite the apparent ease with which many moralise over the prospect of river bathing, a deaf ear is often turned to the fact that the water quality at well-run and maintained swimming pools is still far from clean. Many are indeed *oblivious* to the fact that in Britain, swimming pool water is often over-chlorinated because we British still view the swimming pool as a giant bath. We are not at all comfortable with nakedness and so we do not wash thoroughly before entering the pool, rather we enter with dirty bodies and pollute the water. Chlorine is then added to the mix of pollutants as a body-wash disinfectant. Research by Dr Alfred Barnard[127] into the effects of chlorination on young swimmers (primary school children who swim once every one or two weeks), has led to some disturbing findings. Despite the fact that many authorities hail the indoor pool as

---

[126] The canal has now been restored for navigation.
[127] Leading research at the Catholic University of Louvain, Brussels.

Hung Out to Dry

the only safe place to swim, it is found that when chlorine reacts with organic matter[128] several by-products are produced including nitrogen trichloride,[129] a powerful irritant linked to the destruction of the cell barriers that protect the deep lungs. The damage may be comparable to the effects of tobacco on the lungs of regular smokers. Could it be that this accounts at least in part for the upsurge in the incidence of childhood asthma?

Even with the water heavily chlorinated, health hazards still present themselves. For example, Cryptosporidium causes a severe form of diarrhoea, which infected persons can pass on through the swimming pool. During the year 1999, one hundred and forty cases were reported, which were contracted at swimming baths, not to mention the countless numbers that went unreported. An article in *The Mirror* of November 16th 2000 highlighted the sorry state of our pools. When it is realised that such venues continue to treat users to verrucas, sore eyes, skin rashes, tooth erosion and ear infections, the un-chlorinated water of our rivers proves an appealing alternative. Chlorine may also have a temporary effect on male fertility. The skin absorbs water and it is found that prolonged and repeated exposure in chlorinated swimming baths may lower one's sperm count, a fact worth remembering if fertility becomes an issue!

Regarding the nation's outdoor pools, not all of our lidos have suffered the same fate as those mentioned here. In Penzance, the Jubilee Pool, which was closed for a time, has now re-opened, thanks to an injection of Lottery money, offering swimmers a unique experience. The large slide and the diving platform have now gone of course, but the sizeable triangular pool points out to sea with all the grandeur of an ocean liner. The white-painted walls help to intensify your suntan and there are many floats to entertain the children. In fine style, a fully functioning café provides that touch of refinement that so many lidos now lack. This pool has been fully refurbished and is a real credit to Cornwall. For any one interested in visiting the pool, chapter seven will reveal further delights for those looking for a little excitement nearby.

As we have seen, the popularity and perceived benefits of sunbathing led to the mass construction of lidos throughout the country. Swimming popularity rose to new heights as all began to enjoy cold-water bathing. As more and more people came to bathe, lifeguards became a feature of these establishments and the public's perception of safety in the swimming environment began to

Opposite: London-on-Sea 1939.

---

[128] Such as urine and sweat.
[129] Tear Gas.

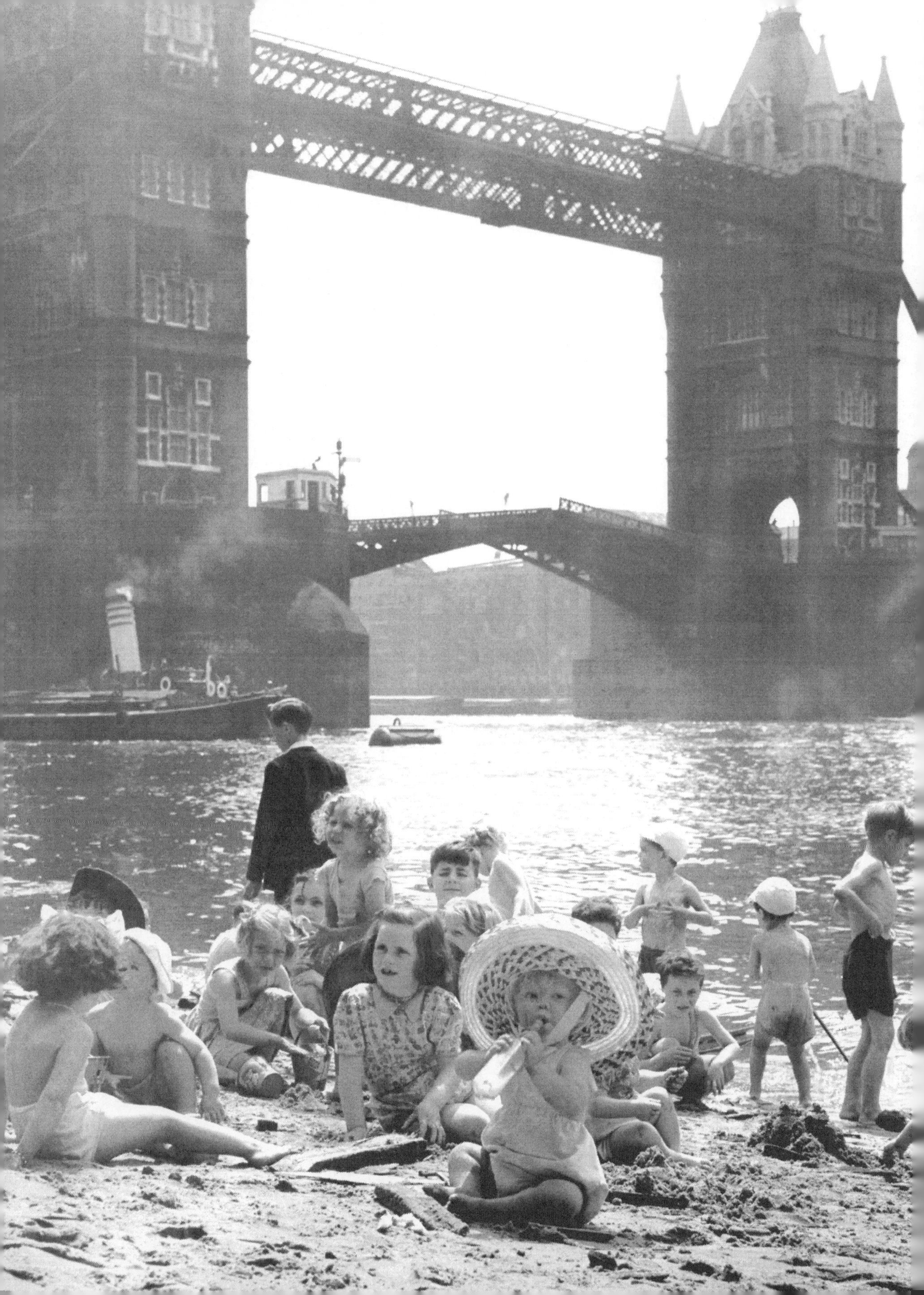

change. The Industrial Revolution transformed the sanitary arrangement of our cities, and as a result, polio came to blight the lives of many youngsters until artificial immunity could be achieved. Meanwhile the rumoured link between water and polio interrupted the enjoyment of swimming for months on end and cast doubt on the cleanliness of natural waters. Ultimately, the British came to see river bathing as dangerous and un-healthful. Natural swimming activities were restricted inland, and unlike the rest of Europe these restrictions increased year by year.

The lido era brought the sexes together in a new and unique environment, changing forever our image of the body. The Victorians had dressed to disguise the human form, but the lido put the body on public exhibition with costumes that left little to the imagination. Between the 1920's and the 1940's, swimsuit fashions, beauty contests, and extensive spectator galleries contributed to a rise in body consciousness. Hollywood portrayed, on the beach and at the swimming pool, a vision of physical perfection to which successive generations have attempted to aspire. The sexualisation of modern society and the commercialism that propels it, rose from the waters of the lido. Thus having considered the many factors that have affected the swimmer:

- the influence of the Romans
- the role of religion
- fears regarding witchcraft
- the advice of doctors
- concerns over morals
- the seaside fashion
- the influence of Captain Webb
- the effect of the silver screen
- the rise and fall of sunbathing popularity
- the opening and closing of the Lido
- the development of British prudery

- let us now look at how all of these influences have impacted on the sport, by turning our attention to the inland city of Leicester. What has happened here has been reflected throughout the country and helps us to better understand the plight of swimmers today. In Leicester as elsewhere, swimmers are barred from open water. Yet, as if the official reason for this has been forgotten (pollution) and despite the fact that water quality in much of its open water is higher than in many swimming pools, the river remains out of bounds to

Lidos Open, Rivers Close

swimmers. In the next chapter you will discover just why this paradox exists and why the swimmer has been 'hung out to dry.'

The author, bathing in the river at Post Bridge, Devon.

Next page: Filled to capacity, the Blue Lagoon at Bristol 1937.

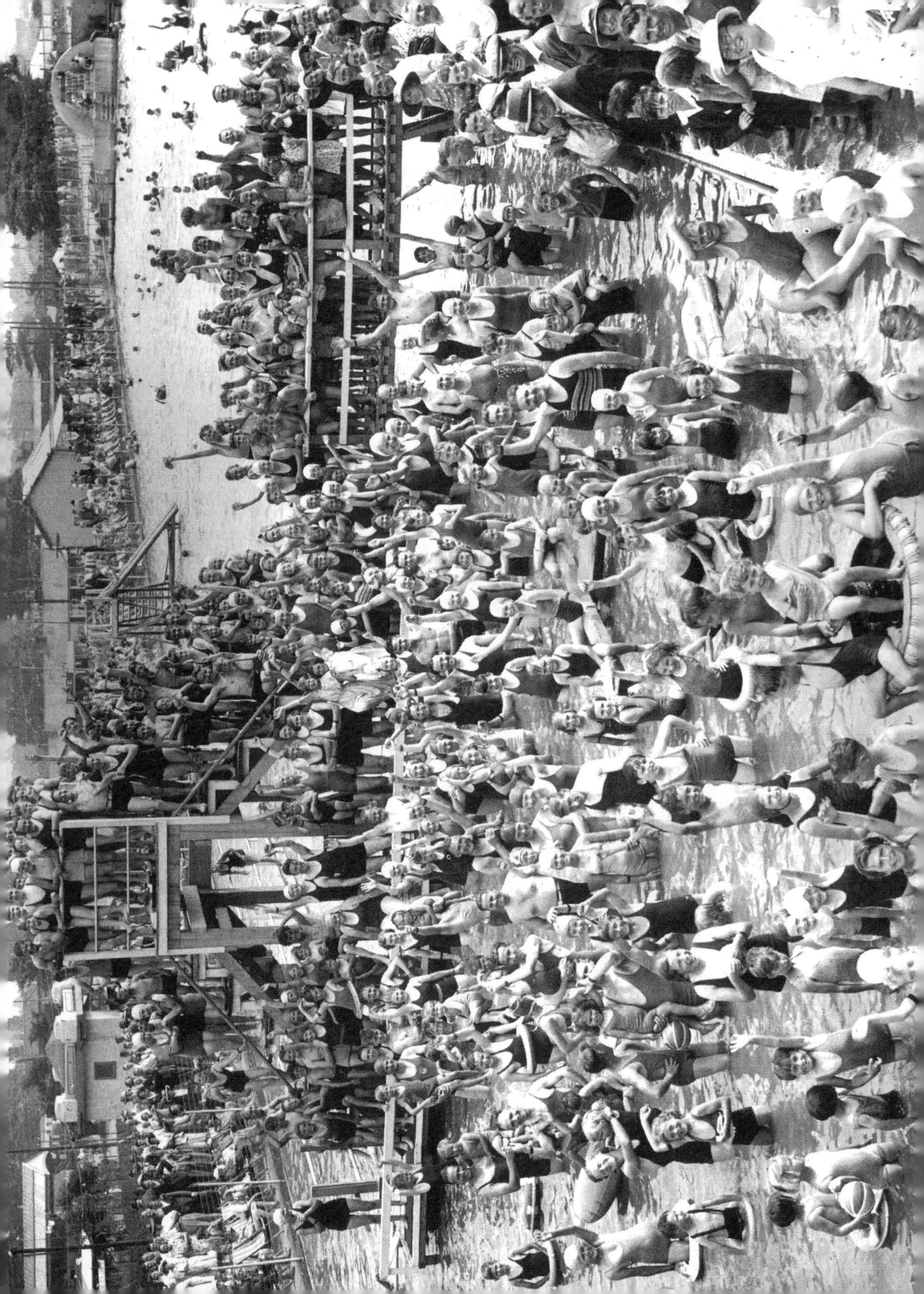

Chapter 6
Leicester: Swim City

You can't get further from the sea in England than the place of my birth, the city in which the conundrum of the British swimmer first came to light. Leicester's relationship with bathing extends over more than two thousand years. Its history is not celebrated, rarely is it mentioned, yet the history of Leicester holds the key to our understanding of why the swimmer has been hung out to dry, and to our understanding the revolution in British culture for which the swimmer is held responsible. Changes experienced here reflect what has taken place all over the country; changes in thinking and attitude that now affect not just swimmers but every individual throughout the nation.

In the middle of the city lies the once hidden remains of its Roman Baths.[130] Ironically these were uncovered during construction work for a new swimming pool, which then had to be re-sited due to its discovery. Opening somewhere around 145-160 AD, the baths provided luxurious hot water bathing for the Romans who settled here. Unlike the larger pool at Bath, Leicester's accommodations were not intended for swimming, but they *were* built in the part of the city that came to be known as the 'swimming quarter'. Roman soldiers would have enjoyed the nearby river for their swimming exercises. As we learned earlier, they equated swimming with reading; both skills being seen as essential. Children were encouraged to perfect their swimming abilities, initially learning with the aid of rush floats. Roman parents (not wanting their offspring to be viewed as ignorant), set an example to the native population, one that would have been followed for generations to come.

What became of the Roman baths in Leicester? Bathing, once celebrated by the Romans, fell from grace due to deteriorating morals. Throughout the Empire, baths came in for condemnation by the Church as attempts were made to stem the tide of hedonism.[131] They came to be viewed as ungodly, as the dwelling place of evil spirits. The Church taught that nakedness leads to sin; washing was seen as ungodly, even demonic. Swimmers also found themselves being disapproved of – for after all wasn't it witches that floated on water? It was in Leicester that the last official 'swimming of witches' was recorded, in 1717. The unfortunate mother and daughter swam like empty barrels floating upon the water though they tried all they could to sink, thus their 'guilt' was

---

[130] Jewry Wall Museum.
[131] Homosexuality was rife.

Hung Out to Dry

supposedly confirmed. So it is not surprising then, that interest in swimming became decidedly bad for your health. Religious conviction and the political union of Church and State ensured that these masterpieces of construction were ultimately closed and destroyed. Additionally, the Anglo Saxon invaders were determined to obliterate their predecessors' accomplishments, and so little is left.

Close to Nature

The 16th century saw a moderation in Church teachings and although the records of history remain silent on the use of the river until 1741, a map of Leicester labels a field in this region as: 'The Bath',[132] showing the return of swimming interest. Daniel Lambert (1770-1809 pictured left) a well-known personality in the town, taught boys to swim here in the river Soar. Lambert was an excellent swimmer and such a celebrity in the town that all of Leicester's youngsters would look to him for instruction. Due to his tremendous size (he weighed over 52 stone when he died and measured 9' 4" around his waist),[133] he could float with ease; in fact it is said that he could swim with two men lying on his back.[134] If some of his charges seemed a little timid, he would carry them across to the bank opposite their pile of clothes and leave them to struggle back. They would then either have to sink or swim!

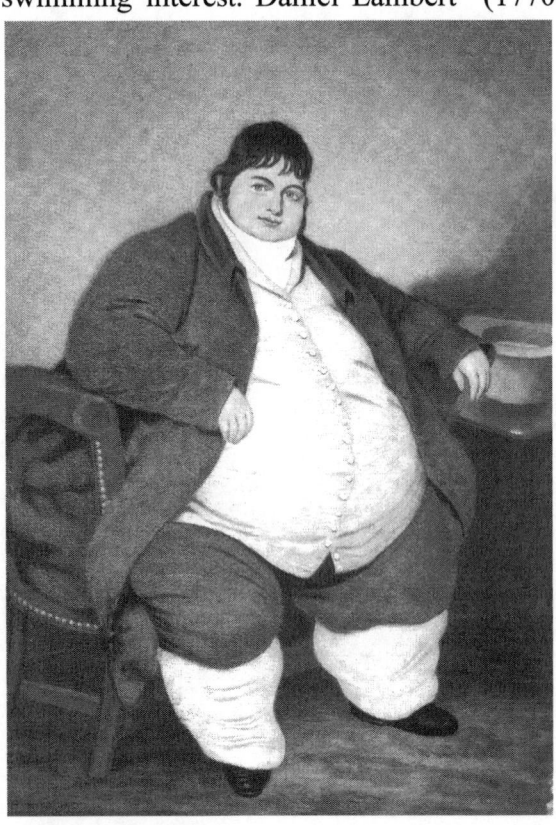

The city's bathing area, originally flanking Bath Lane, seems to have split both north

---

[132] Adjacent to Bath Mill as shown on Roberts' map (possibly 1712)
[133] The Newarke Houses Museum, Leicester displays a number of exhibits relating to Daniel Lambert; clothing, furniture etc.
[134] *The Life of Daniel Lambert* 1892: Stamford Museum.

and south with the growth of the town. Most popular was the area adjacent to Leicester's Abbey, known as Abbey Meadows. The area lies in the proximity of the old Abbey sewer,[135] and the spot finds mention in the *Dare Reports* on working class life in Victorian Leicester.[136] Joseph Dare was a middle class evangelist who did much to assist Leicester's workers to improve their situation and living conditions. Naked outdoor swimming in Abbey Meadows was, though, something of which he vehemently disapproved. He condemned the noisy enthusiasm of those bathing in the Soar and complained: *'Certain classes of roughs can only enjoy themselves by annoying decent people. The bathing in the pasture also deprives respectable females of the pleasant recreation of boating.'*

Despite the area's reputation as a *'dank, diphtherial and febrile spot'*, it can't have been that unattractive if respectable ladies would consider it a suitable leisure area. What *was* offensive, in the mind of the middle classes at least, was the fact that bathers were splashing around in the nude. Dare continues: *'I have seen fellows splashing about up to the North Bridge in full view of the public road and contiguous factories; and other like disgusting exhibitions at the top of Soar Lane coal wharf.'*

It was reasoned that men and boys bathing together in a naked state could be up to no good. Joseph Dare refers to disgusting scenes tolerated in the pasture, whilst others describe the area as *'nothing else but a meeting place for all kinds of vice and filth.'* Something had to be done, so Joseph Wright, the Inspector of Public Nuisances, was sent to investigate. Significantly he reported that there was nothing to complain of, but some could not accept this, concluding that the presence of the Inspector had caused the bathers to moderate their behaviour.[137] It would be improper to suggest that all those attending were of impeccable morals. There may well have been indiscretions, even if not during the Inspector's visit, yet the real problem would appear to be the suspicion and fear that arose out of a clash of culture. The lack of privacy endured by the working class shaped their attitudes; they were without shame. Living in oppressive and cramped conditions with little opportunity for recreation, boys went wild on the riverside; they noisily enjoyed themselves and loved to run and swim naked (they ran to get dry). The middle classes benefited greatly from the labour of these lesser mortals, but their behaviour did not sit well with middle class niceties. The middle class liked everything to be regulated and well superintended, and this was most certainly not the case by the river.

---

[135] Known as the 'Black Hole'.
[136] Haynes: *Working Class Life in Victorian Leicester* 1991.
[137] Elliott: *Victorian Leicester*.

Hung Out to Dry

The success of Leicester's Thomas Cook in providing affordable holiday travel (by train since 1841) had not only contributed to the transformation of the seaside, it had given impetus to the polarization of attitudes regarding public decency on the beach. Back in 1847, Queen Victoria set a new trend by visiting the seaside 'just for fun' as opposed to sea bathing purely for medicinal purposes. Ten years later the Marquess of Westmeath presented a 'Bathing Bill' in the House of Lords requiring men to wear bathing costumes. However, the House thought the subject better dealt with through bye-laws and the Marquis withdrew his Bill.[138] Nude sea bathing came under restriction and inevitably the days for bare bathers at home were now to be numbered. Victorian standards of morality and feelings of British supremacy led to a confidence and determination when it came to dealing with inferiors. After all, Britain ruled one in four of the world's population and clothed the world in wool and cotton. The middle classes had no doubt at all that 'God was an Englishman' and that he favoured the British. They felt that they knew better than the workers and they saw it as their God-given duty to civilise and moderate the potentially dangerous activities of such 'roughs', thereby retaining God's good pleasure. Pressure to conform had its roots in these early expressions of condemnation and it is still very apparent in the area even today, as evidenced by the proliferation of swimming restrictions in the city.

Per Penny per Person

Leicester's first indoor pool was built in the 1840s on New Walk. Warm water fed the sizeable pool from the owner's factory. It was some forty feet long by twenty-one feet wide and was originally available only for private swimming. Things changed, however, when in 1847 the Corporation agreed to pay Mr J P Clarke one hundred pounds towards his expenses and Clarke's baths were opened to the public. This was in response to the government's 1846 directive to provide public baths and washhouses. Leicester then could boast a swimming bath in response to the ruling well before a London pool opened in 1849![139] Bathers (men only) were charged 'per penny, per person, per swim,' and were given a clean towel into the price (costumes were unheard of).

In 1869, the Corporation took over the baths, paying rent to Mr Clarke, and from 1870 onwards children were admitted at half price. Mixed bathing was out of the question and women were only admitted between the hours of

---

[138] *The Times* June 17th 1857. The local act of 1868 enabled the restriction of bathing in watercourses on grounds of danger or indecency. Bathing was thereafter restricted to three places.
[139] St Martins-in-the-Fields. Sinclair & Henry: *Swimming, The Badminton Library* 1893.

8.00 and 12.00 a.m. on a Tuesday, which was of little concession to working women.

Sometime between 1873 (when the building was constructed) and the end of the 1800s, Pick Everard opened his exclusive Turkish Baths at 40 Friar Lane. The dome above the plunge pool is very grand indeed and the pool itself was even used by members of the Baptist Church opposite, as they had no baptismal facilities of their own. These baths enjoyed their heyday around the time of the First World War. They were intended for the upper classes, but many of the officers that frequented the establishment (which developed into a kind of men's club), lost their lives in the trenches. The baths sadly fell into disuse by the end of the Second World War, even though by this time ladies had begun to use them on the one day a week that they were admitted. There was at least one other Turkish bath in the city, nearby in New Street.[140]

Meanwhile, back at the river, men and boys still enjoyed bathing all year round. The problem with Abbey Meadows though, was its openness to public view, compared with the more compact site at Bede House Meadows. Complaints about men and boys bathing nude in the Soar were voiced from time to time; barge women had been afraid to travel through Leicester as crowds of boys would board their boats to dive off and generally make a nuisance of themselves, all of them stark naked. So in 1852 an irate barge woman expressed her displeasure and disgust to the local magistrates, but such complaints were dismissed and like misdemeanours explained away as youthful exuberance even as late as 1871.[141]

Then an explosion of swimming interest hit the nation, with the successful crossing of the Channel by Captain Matthew Webb in August 1875. Throngs of naked boys plied the waterways in response and it all became too much to bear. This same year a new bye-law for the park and St Margaret's pasture was enacted reading: *"No person shall bathe in any water in the park or recreation ground **except** in such place or places specially set apart by the Corporation and may be identified by notice 'Subject to compliance with regulation.' "* Thus nude bathing came under the control of the Corporation, who now prescribed its limitations. No doubt this came as a blessed relief to those who felt it essential to contain the masses of young adventurers. The imitation of Webb saw swimmers spanning great distances up and down river; however the Order would now ensure that youngsters were contained within much smaller stretches of river, out of public view. This would go a long way towards

---

[140] *New Guide to Leicester* 1888.
[141] Richard Rutt: *The Englishman's Swimwear (Costume) ... Annual Report of the Domestic Mission* (Leicester) 1857.

bringing to an end the annoyance and embarrassment experienced by respectable ladies. But it changed forever the thrill of distance swimming; boys and young men had to contend themselves with counting lengths rather than the real achievement of swimming for miles. From this point on, swimmers were in a sense confined by authority and so they paced backwards and forwards like caged animals. In the minds of the prudish Victorians that's exactly what they were. The first victory had been achieved; shameless children were hidden away so that ladies, young and old, could stroll along the riverbank in peace.

Clarke's baths were later re-claimed by the owner and so closed in December 1879. The Corporation was then moved to build their own premises, which opened in Bath Lane in July 1881, but many complained about the waste of public money when outdoor bathing was so readily available.[142] Even so, central government now expected the Corporation to provide swimming facilities and so they had little choice in the matter. However, by opening their own baths the Corporation could take control of the bathing public. To achieve this end, warm water was channelled into the pool from local factories, luring bathers indoors, out of the sight of critics and under the control of the Corporation.

Initially there were plans for four swimming pools in the one complex, two for men and two for women, with an additional fifteen private slipper baths. Women's facilities had taken on great importance, especially following the terrible disaster on the Thames in 1878 involving the *Princess Alice*. In the end, after much delay, the ladies' pools were scrapped and the town had no facilities other than the river for the eighteen months between the closure of Clarke's baths and Bath Lane's eventual opening. The new complex consisted of a circular pool forty feet six inches in diameter and a second pool one hundred and thirty-three feet long and twenty-four feet wide. Six years later, a women's pool finally materialised.

A little later, as Tuke was painting the innocence of boyhood in Cornwall and the ASA were making sure that boys wore swimwear for competitions, concern over the sexuality of children was reaching fever pitch. Boys were being radically circumcised in educated circles to reduce the risk of masturbation, and unruly roughs were being rounded up and drawn into the swimming pool, where their conduct could be superintended. More swimming baths were erected one after another with brand new indoor facilities built: Vestry Street baths in 1891, known by locals as the 'bug bath' due to the prevalence of cock roaches; Cossington Street 1897 (fed by a spring), then in 1901 Spence Street

---

[142] Elliott: *Victorian Leicester*.

Leicester: Swim City

was constructed, followed by Aylestone in 1910.[143] Leicester truly became 'swim city'! So it's no wonder, with all this encouragement for swimmers, that the first long distance river swim through London saw a *Leicester* man Mr J A Jarvis take first place. He raced in the Seine in the 1900 Paris Olympics, becoming the first ever triple gold medal winner. John Jarvis called himself *'Amateur Swimming Champion of the World,'* and he earned 108 international swimming championships to prove it! It is also no surprise that at the first Olympic Games to include female swimmers, Jennie Fletcher of Leicester[144] won bronze for the 100m freestyle. Then at the same games in Stockholm (1912) she formed part of a relay team that went on to win gold. In all, she won over 20 major trophies and titles, becoming champion of England six times as well as setting 11 world records. Her achievements were recognised in 1971 when she was praised as the *'world's first great woman swimmer'*, being included in the International Swimming Hall of Fame. Although she died in 1968 her achievements were not recognised by the City until 2005 when a plaque commemorating her achievements appeared at Cossington Street Sports Centre. These swimmers put Leicester on the map and indeed the city's connection with swimming is truly remarkable.

John Jarvis: 1900 Olympics.

Leicester Shines

What then was to become of river swimming in Leicester? Many factors have played a part over the years as the Leicester Corporation (LC) and later the

---

[143] Leicestershire Records Office (L 797.2).
[144] Born in Belgrave 1890.

Hung Out to Dry

Leicester City Council[145] saw their swimmers leave the waterways. In the north, by 1875, the new bye-law fenced swimmers into an area that now lies directly underneath the by-pass adjacent to Abbey Park.[146] The year 1881 saw the park laid out much as it is today,[147] and sometime thereafter the fencing was removed, with bathers using a sizeable outdoor pool, behind St Leonard's works. The tree-lined St Leonard's baths were well out of the sight of 'decent' people. This pool was to suffer as a result of the popularity of rail travel; it was destroyed as the Great Central Railway ran their line straight through it.[148] It seems ironic that the successes of Thomas Cook, which led to the masses being able to swim at the coast, would ultimately contribute to the destruction of his hometown swimming environment. Due to the growing dependence on the trains, Daniel Lambert's area became extensively developed as Soar Lane Coal Wharf, precluding outdoor bathing in this traditional spot. Bathing in Abbey Park was seen as a nuisance and so in 1904 a bathing station was built beyond the reaches of the park and well out of sight. However, its situation near to the Abbey Meadows Pumping Station made it possible to channel the waste hot water from the engine into the river, in a concessionary effort to warm the waters of the bathing station. An excellent idea in theory, but one that did not prove as effective as was at first thought. The originally steaming water lost much of its gusto on the long journey from the engine to the swimming quarters, which meant that only tepid water found its way into the river and only a trickle at that! Leicester's early swimming history always included warm bath water wherever possible. These efforts show just how interested Leicester Corporation was in times past to encourage swimming, albeit with the motive of containing the activities of the bathers by regulation and control. The new amenity, although somewhat out of the way, did include a concrete river bottom and changing cubicles.

Bathing in Abbey Park was now discouraged except on show days, but on these occasions thousands would travel to Leicester to see the swimming events. They would line the bank of the river to cheer on their heroes in the long distance swims (of both a mile and half a mile). On one occasion, even a solid afternoon of rain failed to dampen the enthusiasm of thousands of spectators watching the proceedings, which were the biggest draw of the show. One thousand six hundred seats were provided for spectators, charged at 6d each.

Leicester had a fearsome reputation when it came to water polo and

---

[145] Leicester City Council replaced Leicester Corporation on April 1st 1974.
[146] St Margaret's Way.
[147] Emery: *The History of Abbey Park Leicester* 1982.
[148] The line was completed in 1898.

these raucous events had a great following. A match against Derby brought a trainload of supporters and with it as much excitement as we see at football matches today. The site of these events can still be identified by the steps in Tumbling Bay, adjacent to the footbridge in the centre of the park.

Water Polo match between Derby and Leicester in Abbey Park, August 3rd 1909; just look at the crowds!

Imagine

In trying to imagine the enthusiasm and zeal that people felt for swimming in those days, football is an excellent comparison. Today, almost every boy enjoys a game of football. Some go on to become famous players; others grow away from the sport but are more than happy to cheer on their favourite team as spectators. The sight of a group of boys playing football in the park brings back to passers-by happy memories of their own youthful joys. It seems scandalous to suggest that football could ever fall from its current pedestal, and yet swimmers have seen *their* sport plunge from pride to prejudice. If signs started to appear reading: 'danger no ball games allowed', under the pretext of protecting children's health, we might react with astonishment. Such restrictions might purport to be for the health and safety of our youngsters, whereas in reality these restrictions would be for the benefit of those objecting to the inconvenience caused by childish joys. As time passed, if football were to be banned completely in our parks, future generations might be surprised to learn just how many spectators the sport at one time attracted, and that it was ever viewed as healthful. If, in an effort to justify their heavy handedness, authorities made mountains out of mole hills, perhaps suggesting that fears of asthma attacks were behind a move to ban football in the great outdoors, we could be forgiven for thinking that excuses were being made up! Yet fears regarding Weil's disease are always trumped out whenever outdoor swimming is suggested, even though the matter has been properly researched and swimmers are found to be less at risk than the general population.[149] Canal water fills Leicester's King Lear's Lake in Watermead Park and windsurfers and triathletes are at liberty to enjoy its waters. Can these regular swimmers really be less at risk than the casual swimmer?

In Leicester, as with other cities in England, if you want to swim with approval you must pay for the privilege and comply with the strict regulations authorities place on the activity. Such has not always been the case. In years gone by, for example, the stream in Leicester's Spinney Hill Park used to be dammed up in the summer to form a swimming pool.[150] In fact, swimming would take place wherever people felt inclined to plunge.

Swimmers usually prefer the company of others and this has always been encouraged as it provides a means of rescue should a swimmer get into difficulties. Traditionally, bathing places have been established for this reason. Baden Powell's words that: *'there should always be a bathing picket posted, while bathing is going on,'* was and still is good advice. But because of our modern day attitudes, swimmers' lives are being put at risk. In Leicester for example, 'NO SWIMMING' signs will generally be placed at even the safest swimming locations.[151] Because of this, swimmers disperse, moving out of public view facing even greater danger should they get into difficulties. Parents feel much happier if their children intend to bathe with others at a recognised spot, preferably one they or the child's grandparents used to bathe at, where the dangers can be identified and prepared for. So it is natural that the bathing places provided by the Corporation in the past proved to be so popular.

Interestingly, both boys and finally girls were admitted to swim at the Abbey Meadows bathing station. Looking back at these early days it's worth noting that swimmers were originally separated by sex, due to concerns over

---

[149] *Environmental Health*, October 1992 page 295: This report covers all cases of the disease between 1982 and 1991, concluding that; 'the risks of contracting the disease and of dying from it, therefore seem to be lower among recreational water sports enthusiasts than for the general population.'
[150] Gill: *The book of Leicester* 1985.
[151] Elsewhere discretion is used; bathers are warned of real dangers.

mixed nudity. Before long costumes were forced onto the backs of all, and yet, as if the real reason for separating swimmers had been forgotten, mixed bathing did not resume for many, many years.[152]

With the indoor facilities provided by the Corporation why did river bathing remain so popular? For many it proved to be a practical alternative to the tin bath in the kitchen; you might remember that even as late as 1950 only 46% of households had a bathroom. Boys especially enjoyed the river, but for girls it was a different matter; they found Abbey Meadows far from suitable. Although members of the United Ladies Swimming Club trained here, they complained that the water was very cold and filthy. This may have accounted for the lack of attendance here as compared with the Bede House,[153] but the main reason lies in the fact that this was not the traditional spot, neither was it anywhere near as attractive a location as was swimming in the park. Parents grant approval to swim at places they themselves know well. Thus, many children continued to enjoy the river in the park, despite breaking the bye-laws, as opposed to travelling to the unfamiliar bathing station where they would have to pay to swim.

The Soar Lane Coal Wharf was changed beyond recognition by Leicester's flood management scheme, but despite discouragement generations of bathers still returned to it like doves to their dovecotes, jumping from the weir and generally carrying on until interest was finally quashed in the 1990s. In Abbey Park, despite vigorous discouragement, the last few cunning children are still to be seen swimming in the traditional place even today.

The Swimming Hole

The Bede House did not move one inch with the flood management alterations and so its tradition and popularity lived on. The weather affects swimming pool attendance both outdoors and in, but the bad weather in 1927 meant that Abbey Meadows only attracted two thousand during the season. Attitudes had changed. Swimming was once seen as an essential exercise, with cold water attracting rather than repelling swimmers. The warmth of indoor swimming facilities changed all of that, drawing people indoors and away from the river. Later, sunlight came to be seen as mankind's new ally on the frontier of improved health. Where better to sunbathe than in the swimming environment? Thus the link between sunshine and swimming unwittingly caused a drain on

---

[152] Pictured in the Leicester Mercury of July 1934, girls swam at Abbey Meadows for the first time.
[153] In 1938 over 7,000 swam at Abbey Meadows whereas 11,000 swam at the Bede House, this despite the 'males only' limitations.

the numbers using such facilities. People now spent more time sunbathing than swimming and they came to feel that it had to be sunny, or else they would not swim (this link has been strengthened even further by the advent of continental travel). However the Bede House had an unfair advantage; not only was it much better developed with jetties to dive from and changing huts provided from early times, but the Corporation also put up a large fence, which enclosed a good sized area of grass for sports and sunbathing. More importantly, the main attraction in later years was the abundance of very warm water that flowed into the canal just upstream from the power station. This stretch of the canal was attractively warm for most of the year. The fish loved it too and it became an angler's paradise. The electricity works built in the 1920s ultimately used eight cooling towers, bringing floods of hot water streaming into the canal. This all went to popularise what came to be Leicester's premier swimming centre. Canal waters today sadly lack the clarity that our predecessors enjoyed. Progress has seen the horse disappear as the motive force of the canal barge, which means that the waters and sediment are currently churned up and dirtied by the propellers of the longboats. But in its heyday the Bede House enjoyed warm clear water.

Looking back, swimmers recall how they use to enjoy the Bede House. A one-armed man, Mr Armstrong, use to supervise the bathing station. Many can remember how he would shout at the boys entering the turnstile, demanding: 'CAN YOU SWIM?' If they couldn't, they were told in no uncertain terms to stay behind the rope marking the shallow area. His stern look warned the boys to behave or else! Mr Armstrong added real character to the place, ultimately being awarded for saving over twenty lives! The water was eight foot deep on the far bank and the painted sign can still be read today (the very sign I used to ponder over when cycling past as a child). It cost a penny to get in, but paperboys got in for free by showing their newspaper bag. The temptation to throw the bag over the wall for others to use led to many illicit swims. Children from the nearby Narborough Road School would escape to the water at lunchtime and then lie out on the grass to dry in the sun. Parents were often oblivious of these lunchtime adventures, as the boys were careful not to ask to take a towel to school.[154] Children especially enjoyed the thrill of diving from the footbridge and hundreds would appear in the summer.[155] The place was alive with boys enjoying the river and sunbathing on the grass; it was always packed, especially on a Sunday. Leicester Corporation encouraged swimming lessons and those school children who passed the 'swimming test' were given vouchers

---

[154] *Leicester Mercury*: May 27 1995 p10.
[155] Colin Hyde: *Walnut Street – Past, Present & Future*.

that allowed them to swim for free at the Bede House. Fathers would bring their sons on the weekend, even in the winter when the station was officially closed, and on Christmas Day there would always be half a dozen that would want to swim the length of the Bede House.

Swimming Days Out

Kenwood, the Jewel of Swim City: August 1968.

Leicester benefited greatly from the two privately owned lidos with which it was blessed, the first opening on August 3rd 1934 at Kenwood, the second at Scraptoft Lane soon after. You will remember that the hot weather of 1928 had set Britons off in a sunbathing craze, and that 1930 saw pioneering nude sunbathers in London spark a riot! Britons were not yet ready for such liberality; yet semi-nude sunbathing was now to be part of the British experience. As a good suntan had now become very fashionable, Kenwood enjoyed huge popu-

Hung Out to Dry

larity, with its extensive grassy sunbathing lawns, high diving boards and attractive semi-circular pool. It was a real attraction during the summer months, being a day trip destination for many of Leicester's population.

Sandra and John Leake enjoy the waters at Kenwood in the 1950s.

Sadly the lido on Scraptoft Lane (the Trocadero) was closed in 1975 and was from then on used by anglers who surely cannot have enjoyed fishing for rainbow trout in these artificial surroundings. The pool was demolished some years later and the area has now been turned into a housing estate. The owner Mr Mark Warrilow said regarding the pool's closure to swimmers: *'There are enough indoor swimming pools in the city to cope with people's needs. Because of inconsistent weather the pool was only being used during a few months of the year.'* The same reasons saw the wonderful pool at Kenwood become a housing estate. The tragedy of it all was that the City did not buy the pool and thus keep it open for swimmers. This is especially true when you consider the fate of its river bathing stations.[156]

---

[156] *Leicester Mercury*.

Danger: Do Not Bathe

Victorian standards for bathing water were a far cry from those of today. Most swimming baths were filled with water which was neither heated nor chlorinated. Bathing charges were highest at the start of the week and fell daily as the water clouded. Baths were emptied, cleaned and refilled entirely at the discretion of the management. They were often filthy, and the bathers weren't much better, with many suffering from skin diseases. Baths were emptied no more than once a week, but often it was more like once a fortnight or once a month. You can imagine the state of the water when hundreds or thousands had attempted to cleanse themselves in it.

In the late 1920s and early 1930s, LC introduced water filtration at all its indoor baths. Then in the August of 1933 the *Daily Mail* drew attention to the deplorable condition of many swimming pools throughout the country. Warnings were given about both the lack of chlorination and its overuse. This article shocked both the public and the medical profession with reports of typhoid and diphtheria contracted in swimming pools. The paper continued to highlight the unsatisfactory conditions, until by 1935 great improvements had been achieved.[157]

As concerns rose over water quality, attention now turned to the Corporation owned river-bathing stations; the Bede House and Abbey Meadows Bathing Station. Dr McDonald, the medical officer of health, reported to Leicester's Sanitary and Baths Committee, that from his bacteriological examination of the waters, he found neither place was fit or would be fit in the future for bathing. The committee decided on Wednesday May 18th 1938 that both bathing stations would close permanently. However, children continued to use these locations along with the rest of the river without ill effect.

Signs were erected on the canal declaring the water unfit for bathing, outlawing a tradition dating back two thousand years. The *Leicester Mercury* (May 19th 1938) reported: *'NEW SWIMMING BATHS FOR LEICESTER AT LAST.'* It said that the closing of the stations had brought things to a head: *'... the Committee have in being an excellent scheme for a municipal open air swimming pool on the most modern lines, which, it is claimed will be as good if not better than any such other pool in the Midlands and a site for this has been tentatively chosen on the Abbey Park road.'* Sadly the idea of this wonderful new pool (proposals for which had been in place since 1930) with its café and pleasantly laid out lawns bushes and trees, was shot to pieces and blown away

---

[157] The 1936 Public Health Act focused attention on water quality. The lake in London's Victoria Park closed and swimmers moved into a newly constructed lido.

by the declaration of war the very next year.

A Long Time Coming

With the condemnation of the river, Leicester now lacked a venue for swimming competitions. The waters were repeatedly tested over the next few years, but hoped-for improvements were elusive. Due to a lack of money, a pool large enough to house spectators was not built until 1966 with the erection of St Margaret's Baths, which were a real credit to the city. A large pool with a diving stage and springboard attracted the interest of nearly all of Leicester's children. Sadly though, a mix up over the measurements meant that the pool was not officially recognised for Olympic competitions a fact that blighted its existence. On entering the complex, swimmers climbed a flight of stairs built over a goldfish aquarium. The view of the extensive pool greeted visitors as they looked through the glass partition at the top. Climbing still further, a large café overlooking the pool was a meeting place for much of Leicester's youth. Behind it, a completely separate pool of shallow depth welcomed many newcomers from city schools to the joys of swimming. Early attendance figures show as many as five hundred and sixty thousand bathers using the facility each year, with twice as many adults attending compared to the older baths. Sunday sessions would attract family groups and often as many as three thousand swimmers would use the bath in just one day. The baths included an extensive spectator gallery and originally it held a number of slipper baths on the ground floor. As times changed, an advanced training pool replaced these facilities. The complete range of amenities ran to a sauna and solarium, providing a range of sessions to suit the needs of all its users. The main attraction of the pool was without doubt its diving stage. Children, especially boys, would flock to the baths seeking the thrill of this provision. The 1988 Health and Safety Commission publication: *Safety in Swimming Pools*, recommended tighter controls when it came to the use of diving boards. This interrupted free access and led to disappointment for many visitors who would only realise that the boards were closed after entering the pool. Partly for this reason, interest in the pool faded, despite the fact that club swimmers still wanted to use it. As children always make up the major percentage of swimmers (up to 35% of pool users are aged between 13 and 17 years, 50% aged 12 and under), it was inevitable that as they stopped using the pool its future was jeopardised. This pool complex was sadly demolished in the year 2000, thus closing the final chapter on the swimming story in Leicester's traditional 'bathing area'.

Back at the river, swimmers continued to use Abbey Park until they were forced out of the water in 1959. The Medical Health Officer reported that the river was polluted to such a degree that it was unfit for bathing, and a prohibition order was enacted.[158] At this time, you will remember, polio fears were at their peak. Even though the link between water and polio has never been proven, fears regarding it were enough to bring the joys of open water swimming to an end. Despite the fact that everyone can now be immunised against the disease, river water is still seen as dirty and dangerous, especially in cities. Although the park keeper enjoyed the river as a boy - as did so many others during their childhood - he came to feel, as a responsible adult, the need to restrict local youngsters from swimming in the river and from jumping off the bridge. He used to sit in his car by the bridge ready to chase away boys enjoying the water on a weekend. Today the whole waterfront is peppered with signs denying people the right to bathe and prickly bushes have been planted on the lawns next to the bridge where the bathers used to lie drying in the sun.

Are these really criminals or just boys having fun? June 1950.

---

[158] E J Emery: *The History of Abbey Park Leicester* 1982 on page 27 he says: 'At the present time, the pollution in the river is still too great for the Prohibition Order to be rescinded, but the future is not without hope.'

Hung Out to Dry

Extremes

The Council have also decided to close the facilities so much loved by younger children; all its city's paddling pools. In speaking with Mr Clive Summerton (Parks Manager for fifteen years), I discovered that there used to be paddling pools in Aylestone Park; Abbey Park; Braunstone Park; Saffron Lane Recreation Ground and Western Park.

The Abbey Park paddling pool was constructed in 1930.[159] Its excellent design, with a large grassed area surrounding the circular pool, made it extremely popular. In close proximity, a sand pit, swings and other play equipment meant that families with young children could enjoy a full day's excitement. Youngsters were always reluctant to leave at teatime, having had as much fun as they would have had at the seaside. The pool used to be re-filled on a weekly basis during the summer season and fi-clor[160] was added to keep the water clean. During Mr Summerton's period of service, he never once received a complaint about cut feet, the major concern of many people. In point of fact, there were never any accidents reported.

Western Park paddling pool was similarly very attractive, but improvements to the children's play area saw the large pool replaced by a roller skating rink (which has since closed), with a new, but smaller paddling pool beside it. The new pool was never as popular; it simply wasn't big enough.

The pool at Braunstone Park was constructed in 1935 and was originally fed by a brook that ran through its centre. The water level in the pool varied with the flow of the brook and it was very popular indeed, situated as it was, in the middle of a council estate. However with concerns over water quality, the pool was halved and kept separate from the brook. Unfortunately the new pool required regular filling from the mains and much more maintenance.

The hot summer of 1995 saw the appearance of blue/green algae in the nearby Rutland Water reservoir. Concerns were raised when animals drinking from the water suffered ill health. To prevent any such danger to Leicester's citizens, it was decided to close all of Leicester's paddling pools, even though contamination was most unlikely in a maintained pool. The chances of such a threat developing in a paddling pool, which is emptied and refilled each week, are in fact zero. This then raises questions over the decision to close the pools. Was it made due to a lack of understanding regarding the issues involved, or did the appearance of algae at Rutland Water prove a fortuitous turn of events for those keen to save money on children's amenities?

---

[159] Opening two years later.
[160] A chemical agent similar to chlorine.

Leicester: Swim City

The Urban Parks Manager, Mr Dayaram, wrote telling me that current health and safety regulations mean that a filtration system would have to be installed before any paddling pool could be re-opened. The equipment is expensive and so none will be opening in the foreseeable future.

The large Western Park paddling pool, July 1969.

Hung Out to Dry

The closure of the Braunstone Park pool, which used to attract a regular attendance of a hundred and twenty at a time on sunny days, has meant that some children now swim in the nearby lake, despite the perils of sharing the same water as the resident swans who hold it to be their own. Most others prudently walk down to the river to bathe.

In conducting my own impromptu survey of the use of the river,[161] I discovered thirty-one children 'illegally' enjoying the water of the canal (11-16 years) and another forty-eight people in the shallower river Biam (aged 2-65). After speaking with these groups I discovered that many enjoyed swimming and bathing quite regularly. The survey was conducted in an area covering approximately half a square mile for a fifteen minute period from 2.00 p.m. The numbers recorded relate only to those actually in the water and did not include those watching on the bank. It seems that in these days of litigation, local authorities struggle to strike a balance between allowing people the freedom to enjoy themselves and being seen to protect the public from danger. However, victory has been achieved in the battle against the swimmer. It is a criminal offence to swim in the canal and river swimming is rigorously opposed in Abbey Park.[162] What is behind this prejudice against open-air swimming? Originally concerns over the conduct and morals of working class bathers saw their freedom restricted to designated bathing areas. Later alarm over water quality forced bathers into manmade pools. Even so, youngsters continued to swim in rivers, lakes and canals until attitudes hardened to the point that prejudice replaced reason and outdoor swimming came under a blanket ban. Clearly the motive for this was concern over public health; yet as water quality improved, the way back for open water swimmers has been blocked by another impediment. A culture of litigation has drifted across the Atlantic from America posing a real threat to business and institutions and especially so as outrageous lawsuits have been upheld by the judiciary. Lawyers have compounded the problem by offering potential claimants the opportunity to take compensation claims before a judge with 'no win, no fee' services being widely advertised. Despite this trend the Daily Mail reported on the 22nd of June 2004 that Lord Phillips, at that time the Master of the Rolls - the second most senior judge in England and Wales - added his voice to those who believe that people should be free to engage in sports which are known to carry a risk and that they shall not be in a position to claim compensation in case of an accident. The judge said: *'I feel very strongly that individuals should **not** be restrained from carrying on sporting activities that involve risk like hang-gliding*

---

[161] July 8th 1999.
[162] Letters from Leicester City Council: July 5th 2011, September 30th 2011.

or swimming' and urged councils not to cave in by outlawing such activities. This is not to suggest that Leicester City Council should encourage open water swimming, but they could knowingly allow swimming without fear of litigation.[163] A refusal to tolerate swimming gives evidence of prejudice towards open water swimmers. The Council endorse skateboarding; providing skateboard ramps and facilities that undoubtedly promote the activity and along with it the risk of being sued. Yet when it comes to open water or wild swimming, despite the fact that no equipment needs to be installed or maintained, the council refuse to tolerate even the idea that swimmers should be given the freedom to return to open water.

Regardless of the amount of 'No Swimming' signs put up near rivers and lakes, people will inevitably continue to swim.[164] Water is especially attractive to children and to stay out of the water on a hot day is both unnatural and, in many cases, impossible for children. Whilst walking by the river I spoke to a group of four boys who had cycled a good distance to spend a summer's day in the water. They had been given the choice either to go to the nearby Leicester Leys Leisure Centre[165] with its exciting flumes and the thrill of bodysurfing in the wave pool, or to spend the day by the river, and their money at the cake shop. Why had they chosen the river? The answer came without hesitation: *'Because there are no rules.'* The boys enjoyed being outside in the sunshine; jumping into the water from the rope swing; seeing the animals and birds on the riverbank and the fact that they could swim outdoors instead of in.

Another group of boys who were decidedly late for their return home took a last plunge and then departed. About an hour later my wife and I came across this group again in another part of the river. When we inquired as to the concern of their parents, they told us that they just could *not* keep out of the water. Surely people have a right to bathe in their local rivers and ponds! It is the responsibility of adults to ensure that children can do so with a measure of safety, which includes removing underwater obstacles and weeds in known bathing areas. This used to be done on a regular basis in Abbey Park prior to the show day canoe event. It was also a regular practice to clean out the model boat

---

[163] Jean Perraton. 2005 *Swimming Against the Stream*, Jon Carpenter.
[164] Sadly, law-abiding people are replaced at such swimming holes with those who care little for authority. This gives open water swimming a bad name, as the behaviour of such individuals proves far from attractive.
[165] Leicester Leys Leisure Centre (fun pool) opened in 1985, a real pioneer with Leicester again leading the way as Swim City. The flume was so popular that a queue of bathers eager to enjoy this new thrill would reach along the wall and all the way to the top of the spiral staircase. The wave pool likewise drew big crowds. The old flume has since been replaced with two longer, more exciting slides.

lake in Braunstone Park, ready for the canoeists. Gravel was spread on the lake bottom to improve conditions for the weekend's activities. Water sports enthusiasts run the same risks as swimmers when it comes to river dangers. Yet we happily tolerate children in canoes, whereas children in the water are seen as unlawful. Surely it is not right to make children feel like criminals, or their parents to feel irresponsible, for allowing them to do what is only natural on a hot summer's day.

A European directive (WFD)[166] is now focusing attention on the quality of our coastal and our inland waterways and lakes throughout Europe. This is good news for swimmers, as it will spearhead further improvements in water quality as all must reach 'good status' by the year 2015. Reductions in chemical contamination (nitrates) washed into rivers from agricultural land will help reduce weed growth. Additionally water treatment works will be monitored and their contamination of rivers curbed, to the benefit of all.

We Don't Want Water...

The Corporation and later the Council have provided excellent swimming facilities for Leicester's people for more than a hundred and sixty years. Extraordinarily, they have pioneered warm water baths from the early days, and they even attempted to warm the water of a river bathing station. Recently a proposal was put forward to build a large outdoor pool, with a good-sized paddling pool adjacent to it, right in the middle of Braunstone Park. This spacious location would have filled the needs of children in local estates; providing just the outlet they needed. This is especially true when you consider that next door to the sun pools, a large competition size indoor pool was planned, along with a diving pool sporting six springboards and five platform diving stages of varying heights, or so the artist's impressions would persuade us. The plan was quashed by local people, partly as a reaction to the closing of a community secondary school that they were unable to prevent, despite the fact that the school was doing well (this cost-cutting exercise was the result of the government's insistence on reducing excess places in schools throughout the country). Locals were incensed and so when the proposal was put forward to build on the park it was rejected and kicked out before the benefits of the scheme could be appreciated. Ironically, the site of the closed school was ultimately selected for the new leisure complex, sadly minus the outdoor facilities. Once the school's demolition commenced, however, opposition erupted and slogans were painted on the perimeter boards screening the site from view. One such slogan: *'Sink or Swim,*

---

[166] Water Framework Directive.

Leicester: Swim City

Leicester City Council, off you go, you ain't getting any of our dough', highlights the fear of residents that some of the Braunstone regeneration money, provided by the government, might be drawn on to fund the project. *'Regeneration, not demolition'* and *'we don't want water, we want bricks and mortar'* again highlighted the true objection; the destruction of the community's secondary school. The objections of the Braunstone community were in fact so strong that they put the future of the project in jeopardy.[167] Although I'm quite sure of the sentiments of yet another slogan: *'The Braunstone spirit will prevail'*, I wonder if the spirit of the local children would have been so firm, had their parents succeeded in quashing the prize of a beautiful new swimming pool. After all, there were no other facilities in this area. In the end, a state of the art leisure complex stunned residents upon its opening. Local children with smiles from ear to ear, stared, open mouthed in disbelief. Two beautiful pools, a first class gym, sports hall, crèche, nursery and café provided leisure facilities, jobs and new hope for the community. Braunstone Leisure Centre offers warm changing rooms, private hot showers and a welcome that is second to none. Initially, admission charges for Braunstone residents were just 40p, a concession made in recognition of the investment made on their behalf. Children filled the pool, enjoying a sense of community. They played under supervision, off the streets and away from mischief. Well done, Leicester City Council!

Recently, this council has revamped all of the City's swimming pools and it would be fair to say that they have been very sympathetic to swimmers over the years, sadly though, Leicester no longer has any diving facilities. Although the new pool has water deep enough for diving, this activity is strictly forbidden for the ordinary swimmer. Originally the new pool was to include a diving stage, but I was told the idea was scrapped, as the diving club was *'just not strong enough.'* Still, it's hard to keep the interest of divers when the only pool with any facilities has been demolished. The nearest venue is an hour away by car, in Coventry. I feel sorry for the club, but even more so for the children; they will miss out the most. Open water natural swimming is also out of bounds and this is something of a conundrum. Now that the river water in the city has returned to the purity it enjoyed in its heyday, there is nothing to prevent swimming restrictions being lifted in Abbey Park. That is, of course, unless the desire to control the bathing public remains seated in the Victorian reasoning that saw the restrictions imposed in the first place.

---

[167] In May 2002 the Government offered to pay for the school to be re-built in its original position. Even so, there was not enough money for the new pool (sadly the Government didn't offer to re-build St Margaret's Baths or Granby Sports Hall also demolished by the City Council). Ultimately Sport England came to the rescue; the pool was opened on December 6th 2004, but regrettably without the diving facilities originally promised.

Hung Out to Dry

The main factor in the demise of the British swimmer is the fact that originally all swam naked. Despite the fact that this may have been considered only natural, the middle classes took it upon themselves to make changes for the better and opposed the naked swimmer. The middle class shaped British culture, establishing and developing the prudery so evident in society today. Their 'tut-tut' attitude brought swift response from young working class bathers who reacted to censure, outraging passers-by with their shameless antics. This clash of culture combined with a desire to regulate and superintend all activities found expression in the condemnation of the bather. At first such censure was brushed aside, but the advent of concern over the sexuality of children led to a public overreaction; swimmers were rounded up and placed into the confinement of the swimming pool. Victorious at their achievement, the middle classes remain adamant that the swimmer should not return to nature, with or without costumes. Prejudice against the swimmer has become institutionalised. As the majority of those who wish to take the plunge are youngsters, it has been easy to shout down their preferences with judgments ostensibly made for their welfare, which in reality are nothing more than controls. Swimmers are seen as a public nuisance. Their presence is unwelcome in public parks and so they are held to ransom in the chlorinated swimming pool.

Environment City

Of course, it is not just in Leicester that restrictions have been imposed. But because of its landlocked location, the improvement in water quality, and because the return of bathing in the city would restore a tradition reaching back to Roman times, there are many compelling reasons to restore the freedom to swim in Leicester. Not least of which, is the fact that as the UK's first environment city, Leicester is in a unique position as a trendsetter for the nation. Fundamental to the environment, water is second only to air, and the city has been keen to regenerate its riverside. I wrote to the organisers, to see if they could be encouraged to reintroduce swimmers to Abbey Park. Unfortunately I did not even receive an acknowledgment. As to exactly what will be done in this regard, only time will tell!

Sadly, the Bede House now lies forgotten next to Leicester's 'Statue of Liberty'.[168] However the water quality of Leicester's rivers has improved massively, and in recognition of this the old signs that read: 'WARNING this water is unsuitable for swimming, DO NOT BATHE', have been taken away. Of course the area is a far cry from the beautiful swimming hole it once was. When

---

[168] Behind the buildings of Leicester Rowing Club and the Watershed on Upperton Road.

Leicester: Swim City

first built it was like an oasis in the countryside, but now it is closed in by buildings on all sides. Later Lady Liberty overlooked the bathers from atop the Liberty shoe factory, but now she has been relocated and she stands with her back to the canal. It seems almost as if she cannot bear to look at the lack of liberty to swim in Leicester these days. For now, swimmers remain at the mercy of those who decide what is best for them. Could it be though, that Victorian prudishness and restrictions are the real reason behind the prohibition today? Or is it just that the Council, along with many others throughout the country, really have no idea just how many people would like to return to the pleasures of open water swimming? The vast majority of swimmers in Britain are children and as such they have no voice in government. Today we do not rejoice to see children enjoying themselves in water; rather we see them as unwelcome in the waters of our parks. Having read the history of swimming on the Serpentine, you will remember that many objections were made regarding the idea of tolerating swimmers in the lake. But when the lido eventually opened, what a success it proved to be! Perhaps the same will be true for swimmers in 'Environment City.' One day I hope the signs that prohibit swimming will be removed, allowing the people of Leicester once again to swim in their own rivers and lakes, in their own parks.

Things have certainly changed over the last century. Whereas people used to enjoy a nearby river or lake as a bathing place, local authorities came to provide 'improved' conditions for swimmers, with both outdoor and indoor pools. Lidos provided a respectable place for sunbathing, and so swimmers left the river to take advantage of these new swimming holes, only to find that when the lidos closed down, their access to the river had been barred. In effect these man-made baths imprisoned swimmers, separating them from the joys of nature. As for the resistant few, those that still swim near to cities, they have been treated with prejudice and branded as criminals so that others do not copy their example. *Dark and Lonely Water* a TV safety film released in 1973, alerted the nation to the near certainty of drowning should a child venture too close to a pond or lake. Parents were terrified and their children had nightmares as the Grim Reaper was shown lurking ready to claim the lives of 'the fool', 'the show off' and those ignoring 'no swimming' signs. Rumours about the dangers of swimming in rivers and lakes ensure that the majority now swim indoors.

When it was realised that the dirty conditions in many of the swimming baths throughout the country were the cause of ill health, effort was made to clean up and sanitise bathing waters. Towards the end of the Century, cleanliness became so important to the British people that they started to raise their children in almost clinical conditions. This separateness from the natural world has created problems of its own, but for swimmers, it meant the closure of nearly all river bathing places. By the 1970s, river swimming had almost come to an end. In many cases the need to leave the rivers was not imagined, pollution levels were simply too high to ignore but, encouragingly, many rivers have seen a great improvement in water quality. For example, in Leicester, the River Soar is now graded as 'good' (B), this is the highest level of cleanliness that can be expected in a lowland river. The levels of bacteria remain moderately high in places, but they do not seem to affect the health of those swimming within the city boundary.

With the development of health and safety awareness we are now seeing a 'cotton wool' mentality dismantle the British way of life piece by piece. Tidal pools at the seaside are having their walls breached to prevent their use. It is argued that lifeguards should always be on hand to monitor such pools, and that public access should be restricted when attendants are absent. The water in swimming pools has to be clear so that rescue is not hampered, and this all makes sense in theory, but seaside pools provide safe swimming away from strong currents and riptides. Destroying such pools leaves the swimmer with no option other than to brave Neptune, yet can it be safer for children to swim in the sea rather than in a tidal pool? The actions of the health and safety conscious are putting lives at risk. Apparently this is not a consideration in the minds of those keen to apply the letter of the law. Regulation rather than common sense throws logic to the wind, regardless of the consequences.

What have we learned from our tour through Leicester's history? We have discovered just why the swimmer has been hung out to dry! Many plausible reasons are offered for the nation's current prejudice towards open water swimming, yet when scrutinised the seemingly watertight logic behind the swimmer's confinement to indoor pools seems to evaporate like a mist. Here in Leicester we have forgotten our swimming heritage; river swimming in Abbey Park remains illegal despite its clean waters and throughout the city our paddling pools remain closed. As for our divers, we have sent them to Coventry! 'Swim City' is not all it once was, but we do have an abundance of indoor pools and children are now encouraged to swim there for free! History suggests that swimming in the great outdoors is a good thing, yet officials advise us that we would be better to swim indoors. This leaves us with the question; is it possible for adults and children to swim safely in the great outdoors?

Thankfully there are still a few places around the country at which traditional swimming survives despite the changes in culture with which swimmers now contend. These pockets of resistance are to be celebrated as they show just what is possible even in this modern world of constraint and officialdom. The final chapter will introduce you to places of outstanding interest for those keen to experience swimming in natural surroundings.

Chapter 7
The Last Stand

Penzance - Cornwall

On the last day of my summer holiday, I visited the Jubilee Pool on the seafront. You may remember reading a description of this pool in chapter five. It points out to sea rather like a majestic liner. Beneath the bow lies the hidden bathing place of the Penzance swimmers. If you walk along the concealed path to the left of the pool, you will find the men's bathing place of yesteryear. This was the retreat of gentlemen only, until the 1950s when costumes had to be donned to allow ladies to join in without embarrassment. Here, enthusiasts launch from a concrete platform, setting off into a swimmer's paradise.

The regulars, some of them quite elderly, take to the sea on a daily basis throughout the year. On my visit, I was amazed to see the bald heads of some of these veterans far out to sea, enjoying their three-quarter mile round trip to the thin metal lighthouse in the distance.[169] Apparently, some of these aquatic gentlemen carry in their shorts a rubber-ring in case of emergencies. In the event that they develop cramp, they can inflate the ring and relax in it, enjoying the view of St Michael's Mount until they recover.

Naturally I wanted to join these swimmers, but I was surprised at Neptune's welcome. On this particular day there was quite a swell which meant, for a first timer, a good deal of trepidation. I did not of course want to find myself dashed upon the rocks, but I needn't have worried, because once in the water I found no current to fret about. The water near the rocks was quite cold, but once a good distance out I found it surprisingly warm and unbelievably blue. The sensation of being carried up and down on the swell of the ocean is something I shall never forget. The water had a soft silky quality that I have not experienced elsewhere. To the right of the pool lies a string of marker buoys the length of a swimming pool apart. Having no partner, I decided to take this route so that I would have something to hold on to should problems arise. Because the entry point at Penzance is so far out, once you begin to swim you get the impression that the sea is miles deep beneath you. As I swam, I thought about those poor passengers of the Titanic so ably depicted by Hollywood, who were marooned with no helper in the freezing sea. I was thinking about these things as I began

---

[169] Gear Pole.

to return to the steps and then realised that a group of elderly ladies had just started their daily swim. The comparison with the Titanic was thus complete as these remarkable personalities swam by, with their heads held high out of the water. Incredibly, they retained their elegance as they rose up and down on the swell, complete with 'shampoo and set' and even dangly earrings. This turned out to be an incredible swim. As I got closer to the rocks I realised that the local children had also come down for some fun in the high tide. These boys and girls noisily threw themselves into the waves, managing to climb out again and again onto the rocks despite the rough conditions. Nearby on the promenade, another group of youngsters were hurling themselves from incredible heights into the sea; an activity that caught the attention of many passers-by. These youngsters, some quite tiny, were already veterans of the sport. Sadly some who venture from high cliffs come to grief, but the attitude seems to be one of 'fait-accompli,' as these young people view every barrier to their activities as just another challenge to overcome, which simply adds to their excitement. It is acceptable if only because it is unstoppable! Inland, such children would mostly come from the rougher parts of town, but here in Cornwall, children from all classes, decked out in wetsuits form an intrepid band of daredevils, mostly boys and all with a love of life and the water.[170]

Just along the coast at Newlyn, local swimmers hold a race each year from the harbour wall to the Jubilee Pool slipway. Further along at Mousehole, the evening's entertainment centred on a water polo match in the harbour: a battle between the sexes. The ladies gained a more than satisfactory triumph. It can thus be seen that Cornwall is a wonderful place for swimmers!

Each summer I visit St Ives and enjoy diving from the pier, especially as we have no diving boards at home. This is a regular high tide sport; and it attracts a large number of local children, as well as the attention of holidaymakers and occasionally even an inquisitive seal!

London

For those wanting to travel back in time, a visit to Hampstead Heath is a must. Open all year round, there are three swimming ponds on the Heath. Firstly there is a mixed bathing pond, with plenty of room for swimmers. It gets very busy in the hot weather, which means that the small lawn becomes covered with sunbathers very quickly. Arrive early if you want to enjoy the sun! The ladies' pond is of course for ladies only and is the best of the three, so I am told. Nearby, the men's pond is very well worth a visit. Do not take valuables with

---

[170] The sea was much calmer on my visit in 2008 and so I added Gear Pole to my conquests.

The Last Stand

you, as when I visited I found no lockers and you are not allowed to take bags into the swimming area. I was surprised to find that the water in this pool was pleasantly warm and I very much enjoyed using the springboard; launching into very deep water. There also used to be a diving tower with a ten-metre board, but this has been removed due to a gradual reduction in the water's depth over the years. Lifeguards patrolled all three ponds. Entrance was completely free and unaccompanied children admitted (provided they could swim) from twelve years of age. Today there is a small charge and, sadly, children now have to be accompanied by an adult until they are sixteen. Swimming here in beautiful parkland beneath the trees is truly an unforgettable experience. Those who try it find it hard to understand why such opportunities are so rare today. The simplicity of the experience connects you to the landscape and the environment in a way that walking or cycling never can. When you enter the water you become one with nature and your fellow swimmers; the envy of passers-by. Children are appalled when parents forbid them to join in and swim in the sunshine.

At the foot of the Heath you will find the Parliament Hill Lido. This is a huge swimming pool, again complete with a springboard. However, the water was a good ten degrees cooler than in the ponds on my visit,[171] due I think to the constant aeration by the fountain and the shallow depth of much of the water. The pool has recently been upgraded and a stainless steel liner now reflects the sun's rays and helps to retain water temperature. Use of this pool is slightly more expensive than the ponds, but it is a wonderful sunbathing area on a sunny day, when it attracts around two and a half thousand happy Londoners. To complete the picture, the Heath also offers children a wonderfully kept paddling pool. I must say this is one of the best examples of co-operation and encouragement for swimmers in Britain. Well done to the Corporation of London!

The Serpentine is also very well worth a visit, but as I have described this historic bathing place in earlier pages, I will just remind you of it here. As a nation we have drawn away from our waters, but here in Hyde Park swimming triumphs as a quintessentially British experience. Spend a sunny day at the lido and you will experience the Big City as never before. You will see for yourself the wisdom of George Lansbury and his endeavours to obtain the right for Londoners to swim in their own Serpentine, in their own park.

Farleigh, Hungerford

The Farleigh and District Swimming Club run the last river bathing station in the country. Camping is available at nearby Stowford Manor farm, which offers

---

[171] 61°f compared to 71°f.

bed and breakfast facilities for those not so keen on sleeping outdoors. This beautiful Tudor house, complete with sloping floors, offers waitress-served high teas to its visitors, and links this bathing area to ages past.

There is a history to the struggle to keep river swimming alive in this region just a few miles outside Bath, much of which is covered in Roger Deakin's book: *Waterlog*. Health and Safety officials paid a visit in 1998 and left their mark by insisting that all the fun things be removed. The diving stage has now been dismantled and a wooden plank is all that's left of the excitement. Sadly, the springboard also had to go, and it seems a shame that authorities feel they have to make decisions for us, rather than leaving people to use their common sense.

The club has more than two thousand members, and the extensive lawns are an ideal venue for swimming parties to enjoy the sunshine. The facilities are somewhat basic, yet the atmosphere is very attractive. Swimming at Farleigh will give you an experience of cooler waters and reveal to you the benefits of cold water open bathing. The water is regularly tested to make sure it reaches the high standards required of a bathing place open to the public (quality B). Here you can bathe with confidence.

Nearby in Bath, the old Roman swimming pool has been closed to adventurers since 1978. In the period following the Second World War, the old Roman swimming pool was open to bathers for two weeks during the Bath Festival. In the evenings, swimmers enjoyed a dip in Roman style, followed by a meal in the Spa complex. The NHS pulled their subsidies to spas in 1976, and then two years later, the alarming discovery of a bug that appeared in the water from time to time was considered such a health hazard that it brought this historic experience to an end.[172] The Council felt unable to intervene because of capital restraints; thus the combination of chronic under-funding and the health scare put an end to all of the spas in Bath. The good news is, that in 1983 a borehole sourced water from greater depths for the taproom, so that those wishing to taste the spring water can now do so safely. The taste is medicinal in quality and there are always plenty of nearly full glasses scattered around, which tells you something about its flavour. A new complex has now opened with assistance from the Millennium Commission, so bathers can once again take to the waters, with blessed relief for those suffering from sports injuries, rheumatic pains, sinus-related ailments and skin problems, with rooftop bathing in the open air. Unlike Roman times however, these experiences do not come cheap. The old Roman swimming pool remains out of bounds to swimmers, but at least it is now possible to get wet in Bath!

---

[172] Amoebic Meningitis present in all hot springs.

The Last Stand

The star attraction: Henleaze.

Henleaze Swimming Club

'Never swim in quarries!' Those words were chanted repeatedly throughout my childhood: 'the water is far too deep and freezing cold' we were warned. Even though my experience of swimming in such places has been somewhat restricted, I must say I have not found the water to be as cold as I had been led to believe. On Hampstead Heath you will remember my saying that the bathing ponds have water temperatures that are much higher than in the nearby lido. There are other problems of course: sharp rocks just under the water's surface (but not on the Heath) and difficulties in finding somewhere to get out. Who then would have thought that a swimming club could have been successfully operating from just such a venue since 1919? Remarkably, Henleaze Swimming Club is not just still open, it's thriving!

    I was invited to Henleaze Lake on a sunny August Saturday, and arrived to find Britain's premier open-air swimming attraction operating in full swing. The club owns the old quarry outright (Lake Road, Bristol); however, one of the conditions of purchase was that it should *not* be used for swimming instruction. This is because there are no shallows at the lake whatsoever; and so all members must prove that they are capable swimmers before they can join. The two youngest had proved their mettle earlier in the season by swimming for 50 metres unaided under the watchful eyes of a club official. The twin girls, just four and a half years old, now regularly enjoy the lake along with the other one thousand three hundred and sixty members. Before you decide to rush off to Bristol for the weekend however, I would point out that one of the biggest problems facing the club is its very popularity. Car parking is limited and even if all the members walked to the lake, there is a limit to the number of people it can accommodate. There is a waiting list for those yearning to join and if you are prepared to wait patiently, then you can send a SAE to the club and ask to join the queue for membership, but don't hold your breath. The club is not open to the public, and sadly therefore, you cannot visit just for the day (this is because of the high numbers attending the lake already). Young children are excluded out of fears for their safety and all in attendance now have to truly be swimmers. At most quarries there are signs reading: 'DANGER, KEEP OUT, NO SWIMMING.' What a contrast to find a disused quarry for: 'SWIMMERS ONLY' where it is non-swimmers that must KEEP OUT!

Henleaze has been described as a secret garden and as a time capsule. It is reminiscent of Henley-upon-Thames and is in fact a remarkable place. The sign on the main road spells out its attractions: 'Swimming; Diving; Sunbathing and Fishing.' The focal point is without doubt its diving stage, with its three platforms and two springboards. Even those who do not intend to use the diving tower, find the sight of brave young things launching themselves from it quite irresistible. Children can attend unaccompanied once they reach thirteen years of age, and with this terrific diving facility I can imagine your concluding that scenes of mayhem and abandon must run rife. Yet that is not the case at all, rather the opposite, as youngsters grateful for the amenity display a great deal of level headedness, especially when using the diving equipment. Unlike a swimming pool environment, people are expected to look out for each other, supervise their own children and behave in such a way that others are neither inconvenienced nor put into danger. Can it be true that people today are acting in such an unselfish way? The superintendents at the lake are nothing like the 'commandants' of many indoor pools. They are there ready to give assistance if required, but I didn't hear one whistle blown, or even a raised voice during the entire day of my visit. The dangers of swimming in a disused quarry are drilled into all new members, with the result that problems are few. At the gate it is a different story, access is strictly limited to members only and there is no bending of the rules. The club carries an excellent safety record, and they will not have it ruined by intruders, however insistent they might be.

The club has not been without its problems. Although the lake was used for swimming and diving competitions from the outset, changing times saw measurements become more critical, rendering the lake imprecise by comparison to man-made pools, not to mention variations in water temperatures and the difficulties in marking swimming lanes. As indoor pools sprung up in Bristol during the sixties, children got used to much warmer swimming waters, so that by the seventies they simply would not swim in cold water any more. Then in 1988 the Health and Safety Commission published their book: *Safety in Swimming Pools*, setting out minimum recommended depths of water below high diving platforms. Although there had never been any problems with diving from the ten-metre board, if an accident were now to occur and the recommendations had been ignored, the club might well be accused of negligence and so the highest board was closed. Despite the fact that official swimming competitions were suspended for a long time at the lake,[173] it survives as a swimmers' refuge, surrounded by houses and hidden like a shy oasis amid the trees. The water quality here is excellent; spring water in fact. No wonder it proves to be such an attraction.

This swimming club offers its members excellent facilities with clean, well-maintained toilets and showers. The ladies get changed in a fully renovated WWI First Aid Post. The gents avail themselves of more spartan facilities: a screened-off area with covered benches.

There are two concerns that open water-swimming presents to all, however careful they may be: blue/green algae and Weil's disease. The Environment Agency has come to the rescue regarding the algae. They recommend that small quantities of loosely packed barley straw be submerged just below the water's surface in lakes, rivers and ponds. As the straw begins to rot, it releases chemicals that inhibit algal growth. At Henleaze, I noticed a number of stockings stuffed with straw floating near the surface. This simple solution is remarkably effective, inexpensive and easy to apply. The straw remains effective for six months, so only needs to be replaced in the spring and autumn.

Weil's disease is not an issue at Henleaze. The problem is overcome by calling in professionals to deal with any curious rats. Rentokil have placed a number of metal boxes around the lake containing rat poison. I think the local rat population have got wind of this, as they seem to be very reluctant to visit.

---

[173] In 1998 the Gloucester County Open Water Championships were held at Henleaze. This became an annual event with seniors swimming 2000 metres and juniors 1000 metres.

Hung Out to Dry

I was very sorry to leave Henleaze at the end of the day. The two springboards along with the 5m and 7.5m platform had proved to be an exciting entertainment. I envy those living nearby who find that membership adds more than a little sparkle to their lives. Henleaze is living proof that open water swimming can be safe, diving need not be dangerous and people can act sensibly. Is Henleaze really a time capsule, or is it more likely to be a window on the reality that swimmers have not changed all that much over the years? Despite the influence of the Health and Safety Executive,[174] fun in the sun is still available in Bristol, due in no small measure to the determination and resilience of a small group of dedicated committee members.

Cotswold Water Park

From the foregoing you might be tempted to think that it would be possible to resurrect many of the bathing places lost in the course of recent history. The fact is that our culture has changed unrecognisably over the last hundred years. Modern concerns over water quality, health and safety are not going to evaporate overnight, and nor should they. Even so, bathing in the great outdoors should not quickly be dismissed as impractical. It truly is possible to marry our modern concerns for hygiene and safety with our desire to swim in a natural environment.

Opened in 1981, the beach at Keynes Country Park[175] is a practical example of just what can be achieved when the desire to provide such facilities is strong enough to overcome the first few obstacles. Advertised as the Children's Bathing Beach, one of the many disused gravel pits that make up the Cotswold Water Park[176] has been developed into a leisure area that families can enjoy in safety. The swimming area is clearly defined with shallow water near the beach, gently shelving to about six feet below the wooden boom that separates swimmers from the rest of the lake. Lifeguards are on duty, keeping a watchful eye on the proceedings. Their periodic announcements over the tannoy are the only reminder that we are still in good old England. The beach itself consists of rounded pea gravel and sand; the water remains mostly clear and pleasantly warm. Barley straw is employed to avoid any possibility of algal development, and rodent control dispels fear over other undesirables. Thankfully, beyond the

---

[174] The HSE was established to assess risks at work, yet it has spread its influence to a much wider field. Although it only officially offers advice, the current trend is to take its word as 'Law'.
[175] Cotswold Country Park.
[176] The largest area of man-made lakes in Europe.

boom a wire mesh restricts the movement of fish, keeping them out of the swimming area. Some of the fish are bigger than many of the children who bathe here! The water quality is regularly checked by the Environment Agency, and by way of final reassurance, a large blue flag (clean beach award) waved in the wind adjacent to the lifeguards station up until 2004. Since then it has not been applied for partly due to the high costs involved.

How has all of this been paid for? At first simply by charging people to park their cars near to the lake, whereas now *individuals* pay as they enter the complex.[177] The popularity of the setting ensures its success. Adjacent to the lake, play areas delight the children; a shore side café revives the adults, and a visitor centre gives the whole place a holiday feel. Although it is possible to use other water areas nearby for canoeing, sailing, windsurfing etc, the vast majority of visitors arrive with cars brimming with inflatable boats, deckchairs and play equipment. They head for the beach, which fills to overflowing. The children play happily, enjoying the water whenever the sun shines.

If anyone doubts that open water swimming is practical for today, I would encourage them to visit this water park to see firsthand just how we as a nation are missing out on what nature has to offer!

---

[177] The amount varies with the season but children are always very much discounted.

In Conclusion

We have seen many changes in the swimmer's fortune over the last two thousand years. The pendulum has swung the swimmer in and out of favour, with various concerns being expressed regarding those who venture into open water.

Britain has been largely responsible for the worldwide acceptance of swimming in this modern age. The invention of the seaside holiday and the moral concerns over bathing costumes and/or the lack of them, all originate from our land.

The current climate finds river swimmers in the minority. Local authorities fear that reprisals in the form of litigation will result from tolerance, and so many bar swimmers from waters in public view. Nearly all of Britain's diving boards have been sacrificed on the altar to the god of health and safety, so many youths (who seem to thrive on the thrill of risk-taking) seek out quarries and high bridges from which to launch themselves, because there is simply nothing else available.

Like me, you may have been surprised to see so many naked swimmers in the photograph of Victoria Park, London. Realising the very modern nature of swimwear, I have no doubt at all that such youngsters would be far from impressed with the outfits they would be expected to wear today. Perhaps, it is not the lack of costumes years ago that should astonish us, but rather the changes that have brought such freedoms to an end. The Victorian adage: *'children should be seen and not heard'*, has now been taken a step further. With the proliferation of paedophiles ready to prey on young children (or so the press would have us believe, see page 83 and footnote 91) and the changes in the way we British now view the body, children these days are far from comfortable at the thought of even being *seen*! After conforming to the middle class dress code, young working class bathers, having put on their costumes, find themselves chased out of open water altogether.

Middle class children still enjoy our rivers and lakes; swimming and diving, whilst sailing and canoeing. Working class children have no such advantages. When they attempt to join in the fun by bathing in open water, their actions come in for scrutiny and suspicion. So youngsters look for out of the way places to enjoy the water; they are being forced out of sight and into danger.

A new craze for wild swimming guidebooks is being well received by the nation, reawakening appreciation for the great outdoors. Adventurers looking to recapture the joys of open water swimming are directed to out of the way beauty spots where they can enjoy a dip in an approved, if isolated location.

The Last Stand

Devotees follow their new *Baedeker* to the shores of a refreshing pool, lake or river and many experience cold water bathing for the very first time.

Great Britain once led the world as a swimming empire. As the British did, so the world followed. We were once proud of our swimming tradition and of the huge numbers of youthful swimmers that thronged our waterways. As a result the health of the nation was greatly improved by its devotion to water. Swimming pioneers such as Captain Matthew Webb, John Jarvis and Jennie Fletcher, and a host of poets and artists throughout the country, brought fame to our nation and healthy exercise to its people. Now we set a different trend by frowning upon open water swimmers. Yes, we say, it would be nice to be able to swim outdoors instead of in, but as a nation we think we know better. We imagine that river water is dirty and the cause of all manner of ills. We developed an aversion to cold water once peculiar to the fairer sex, thus spelling doom for the British seaside. Yet does it really matter that the swimmer has been hung out to dry? Why not ask the current generation of obese, allergy-ridden youngsters? Ask the children who find themselves under virtual house arrest resulting from perceived fears over their safety. Today the swimmer confined to indoor facilities, swims in disinfected water containing health hazards of its own. In many areas, would-be 'wild-swimmers' are virtually criminalized for acting out their desire to swim in the great outdoors. Yet those who are still free to swim in the open every day of the year find their lives immeasurably improved because of it. Their bodies glow as they emerge from the water, resistant to disease and fortified against depression.

Looking back over the photographs of this book, surely you cannot help but notice the major reason for swimming popularity? The plain fact is that swimming is fun! Yes, swimming is good for us. It's good for our health, the perfect exercise for old and young alike. Do we really have the right to bar people from using rivers and lakes when wild swimming is so good for us? It is true that there are many indoor facilities available today and swimmers appreciate and enjoy these amenities, but painters and poets do not depict swimming in such pools, do they? This is because they are far from idyllic locations. Rather, indoor pools are a legacy of the Industrial Revolution, a compromise, a concession and a confinement that bears no comparison to swimming in natural surroundings. Authorities want to pluck the last of us out of the water, but frankly we don't want to come out. There is no doubt that the war against the swimmer has been won. The Great British Swimming Empire lies in ruins and the swimmer has been 'hung out to dry'. Battles have been fought and lost and our culture has been completely reshaped in the process. Can anything be done to resurrect the joys of open water swimming? As we have seen, swimmers have had a chequered history. Times and cultures change, authorities are replaced, and

Hung Out to Dry

swimmers will be ready to return with the changing tide. The swimmer may have been hung out to dry, but somehow our costumes keep getting wet.

Despite the restrictions, boys still want to have fun
Leicester 1998.

Credits

Front cover, 10, 29, 38, 50, 56, 87, 111, 114 Getty Images.
6, Sexby 1898: *The Municipal Parks and Gardens of London.*
9, 31, 74 Ayriss, Lucy
12, 13, 17, 23 anonymous Sinclair & Henry: *Swimming; The Badminton Library* 1893
26 Dodd S T
32 MGM
33, 90, 113 Ayriss, K J
57, 149, 152 rear cover upper: Ayriss, C R
37 Marshman, Joan: *Bristol Evening World;* reproduced by kind permission of the trustees of Henleaze Swimming Club, Bristol.
60, *Punch* 1870.
62, Heath, William c1829
63, 67 Photographer unknown
65, 116 Wikimedia Commons
68 grateful thanks to Mr D Bell
70 Paragon
73 Partridge Bernard: *Punch* 1898
84 United Artists
92 Masterman, A T
101 Photochrom Co Ltd
106 Microsoft Clip Gallery
121 *La vie au grand air* 1900
123, 131 Emery, E J: *The History of the Abbey Park Leicester* 1982
127, 133 courtesy of: *The Leicester Mercury*
128 Leake, H
145 Klemperer, Derek; reproduced by kind permission of the trustees of Henleaze Swimming Club, Bristol.
Rear Cover lower Ayriss, B C

Bibliography available online at: www.hungouttodry.co.uk/page46.htm

Special thanks go to my dear wife for translating my dyslexic scribbling into legible text.

Reader's responsibility: Whilst every effort has been made to ensure the accuracy of the information presented in this book, anyone who decides to swim in open water should remember that this is not entirely without risk. Neither the author nor the publishers will be held legally or financially responsible for any accident, injury, loss or inconvenience sustained as a result of the information or advice contained herein.

Hung Out to Dry

A

Abraham	48
Adam & Eve	41, 75-6
Æthelberht King of Kent	16
afterglow	58
air bath	79
Akemanceaster	15
alcohol, danger when swimming	103
Alfred the Great, King of Wessex	16
algae, blue/green	132, 147
allergy's	151
Amoebic Meningitis	144
anglers, equally at risk	107
Anglo Saxons	15, 116
Aquae Sulis	15
Armstrong, Mr of Leicester Bede House	126
ASA	23, 66, 120
Assyrian swimmers	12-3
asthma	101, 110, 124
Augustine of Canterbury	15
Augustine of Hippo	41, 51, 75

B

bacteria, water quality	140
Baden Powell, Robert	28, 49, 72, 124
baptism	16, 42, 76
barley straw, inhibits algal growth	147-8
Barrie, Sir James	94
Bath Lane baths, Leicester	120
Bath, City of	12, 14-5, 19-20, 27, 44-5, 55, 116, 144
Bathers, painting by Henry Scott Tuke	65-6
bathing machines	20, 61-2, 64, 66-7, 85
bathing, mixed	13-4, 41, 44-6, 63-4, 67-8, 97, 118, 125, 142
bathrooms	44, 67, 125
Beach Hut	64
Beal, Benjamin	20
Beckyngton, Bishop	44
Bedale, Dr	23
Bede House, Leicester	125-9, 138
Bekkers, Dr	47
Bible	39-40, 43, 47-8, 53, 75-7
Black Death	44
black smoke, public health act	80
Blackpool	57
bladders, swimming aid	17
Bladud, Prince	14
Blood, Colonel	18
boarding houses	69
Bourne Bottom	59
Bournemouth	59
Braunstone, Leicester	132, 134-7
breaststroke	21-2, 28
Brighthelmstone	20
Brighton	20, 59, 63
Bristol	36, 106, 113, 145, 147-8
British culture	66, 71, 77
British Empire	21, 30, 36, 53, 78, 151
British Swimming Club	64
brothels, bathhouses	44
Bubonic Plague	44
Bubwith, Bishop	15
Burgess, T W	23
Butlin's Holidays	34, 69
Buxton	12
Byron, Lord	21

C

Caer Baden	15
calecons	67
Cambridge	16-7, 21, 67, 92
canal, swimming	7, 71, 102-3, 108, 126, 129, 134, 152
cancer	71, 75, 89, 102
canoeing	107, 135, 149
Caracalla	13
Carry on Camping, (1968)	84
Celts	14
changing areas for swimmers	62-3, 72, 91, 95-7, 122, 126, 137
Channel swimming	23-4, 119
Charles II, King	18, 45
Cherwell, river Oxford	16, 91
chlorination, effects on swimmers	109, 129
chlorination, lack of	129
chlorination, lake water	97
Christianity	16, 40, 53
circumcision	46-9, 85, 120
Clacton-on-Sea	59

Index

Clarke's baths, Leicester 118, 120
cleanliness 15-6, 22, 39, 40, 44, 48, 53, 139
clouties 57
coal strike (1921) 80
cola and tummy bugs 108
Colchester 64
cold water
   aversion today 147, 151
   bathing 19, 125, 144
   cure 18, 55
   ordeal 43
   benefits 58
   bodies reaction to 27, 51
   effect on body 18, 49, 104-5
   precaution against immorality 42
Constantine, Emperor 42
continental holidays 33-4, 89, 103, 126
Cook, Thomas 57-8, 118, 122
co-ordination dyslexia swimming 35
Cornwall 57, 120, 142
   Falmouth 66
   Fowey 104
   Hayle 100
   Penzance 110, 141
   Polruan 104
   Portreath 21
   St Ives 4, 142
Cossington Street baths, Leicester 120-1
costume, swimming 8, 19, 55, 61, 63, 67-71, 78, 84, 91, 95, 118, 125, 138, 141, 150, 152
crime rise due to reduced amenities 100
Cromwell Oliver 52
Crusades 51
Cryptosporidium 110
Cuckoo Weir, Eton school 105
culture 9, 36, 46, 49, 52-4, 72, 75, 77, 85, 88, 115, 117, 138, 148, 151

D

D'Arblay, Madame 20
Daily Mail campaign, water quality 129
Dames' Delight, Oxford 91
Dare, Joseph Leicester 67, 117

dawn swim 19, 58, 90, 94, 97
day trips origin 57, 60
De Arte Natandi 17
Defoe Daniel 19
Denmark, beaches clothing optional 72
devices, swimming aids 22
Devil
   bathers likened to 16, 42-3, 53
   swimmers likened to 44
Digby, Everard 17
diphtheria 129
distance swimming 21, 24, 120, 122
diving 7, 21, 32-3, 36, 74, 91-2, 94, 97-105, 110, 126, 128, 130, 136-7, 140, 142-4, 146-8, 150
drowning 11, 17, 24-5, 27, 31-2, 36, 39, 102, 104-5, 108, 139
ducking of witches 43
dyslexia and swimming 35

E

early morning swim 58, 90, 94, 97
eau-de-cologne replaced washing 16
Eden, expulsion from 41
Eden, garden of 41, 75-6, 84
Ederle, Gertrude (Channel swimmer) 24
Education Act 30
Education Authorities dyslexia 35
Education, Board, swimming (1891) 30
Edward VII, King 28
Egyptians 11, 75, 77
Elizabeth, Queen 16
Emmanuel College, Cambridge 21
Encyclopaedia Britannica of 1797 21
Environment Agency 108, 147
ergotism and witchcraft 43
Eton, school 67, 104
Ezekiel, Bible book 40

F

Fabian, Leo 96
Falk, Bernard 78
Falmouth, Cornwall 66
Farleigh, river swimming club 143
fertility and Chlorine 110
fi-clor, use in paddling pools 132
filtration swimming pool water 129

155

Finland, culture	72
Finsen, Nobel Laureate	78
Fletcher, Jennie of Leicester	121, 151
Floyer, Sir John	18
foot shower	72
football, comparison with swimming	51, 93, 123-4
Footlight Parade, film (1933)	32
Forsberg, Gerald	94
Fowey Cornwall	104
Fraser, Alexander	45
Frei-körper-kultur	80
frog as swimming instructor	21
front crawl, swimming stroke	12, 22
fun pools	34

G

Gentleman's Magazine (1769)	20
George III, King	20, 24, 59
George IV, King	20, 59
George V, King	95-6
Germany, culture comparison	25, 72, 77-8, 80-1, 85
Glasgow pool attendance records	30
Goldring, Douglas	95
Greek culture	48, 75, 77
Gregory I, Pope	15
guilt, intrinsic to British culture	46, 71
gymnasium, Greek	75
gymnasium, Roman	13
Gymnosophists	69, 81

H

Hadrian, Emperor	14
Hampstead Heath, London	93, 103, 142, 145
Hardman, William	64
Hayle, Cornwall	100
Health and Safety Commission	33, 130, 147
Health and Safety Executive	148
health and safety regulations	99, 123, 133, 140, 144, 148, 150
Henleaze Swimming Club	36, 145
Henry I, King	15
Henry IV, King	16
Henry VIII, King	17, 45
Hitler, Adolf	81
holiday camps	69
holidays	34, 36, 55, 59, 60-1, 63, 69-70, 77-8, 88-9, 98, 118, 149, 150
Hollywood	32, 84, 112, 141
homosexuality	14, 46, 84, 115
hospitals and cleanliness	102, 108
hot water', 'getting into	42
hotels & bathing facilities	44
Houghton, Fred	94
Hyde Park, London	4, 24, 39, 69, 93, 143
Hydrotherapy	55

I

immersion, total baptism	42
indecent exposure	64, 95
indoor pools, lack of profit	100
Industrial Revolution	12, 52, 60, 66, 74, 80, 85, 112, 151
inspector of public nuisances, Leicester	117
Institute of Baths Management	34
instruction, swimming	11, 31, 83, 126, 146
Internet and child pornography	82
Isaiah, prophet and bible book	76

J

James I, King	43
Japan	46
Jarvis, Mr J A swimming champion	24, 121
Jerome, Church father	39-41, 75
Jesus, Christ	40, 42, 44, 76
Jews	48, 49, 77
Julius Caesar	11

K

Kellogg, John Harvey (cornflakes)	46
Kenwood, lido Leicester	127, 128
Kenworthy, Harold	22
Keown, Eric (Punch)	96
Keynes Country Park	148
Kilverts, Parson	64
Knitted swimming costumes	68

Index

L

Lambert, Daniel	116, 122
Lansbury, George	95, 143
Leicester	5, 7, 22, 24, 36, 57, 67-8, 102, 112, 115-140, 152
Abbey Meadows	117, 119, 122, 124-5, 129
Aylestone baths	121
Bede House	119, 125
Kenwood Lido	127
regeneration, Braunstone	136
St Margaret's Baths	130
Turkish Baths	119
Lewis, C S, loved Parsons Pleasure	91
Leysin, Switzerland sun clinic	79
lidos	33, 39, 69, 90-103, 110, 112, 127-8, 139, 143, 145
lifeguards	28, 100, 103-4, 110, 140, 143, 148-9
lifesaving	17, 22, 24, 27, 31, 104, 140, 147
litigation, fear of	33, 134-5 150
Liverpool	57
London	4, 7, 16, 21-2, 24, 44, 46, 59, 81, 93, 96, 103, 109-10, 118, 121, 127, 142-3, 150
Hampstead Heath	103, 142, 145
Parliament Hill Lido	143
Serpentine	4, 24, 27, 93, 95, 139, 143
Victoria Park lake	7, 23, 26, 93, 129, 150
London-on-Sea	109
Long Bridges, Oxford	92
longboats and water quality	126
Longfellow Wilbert	32

M

Maecenas Gaius	11
Man and Sunlight, Hans Suren (1924)	80
Margate	20, 59, 62
masturbation	47-9, 85, 120
McDonald, Dr medical officer	129
Merry-Go-Round, BBC sex education	86
middle class	39, 46, 48, 51-2, 54, 59, 61, 63, 66, 69-70, 73-4, 85-88, 117-8, 138, 150
Midland Counties Railways, tours	57
Minerva, Roman deity	15
missionaries and culture	52, 88
modesty hoods and bathing machines	62
monks of Bath	15
morals and swimming costumes	55
Music Hall, seaside	24

N

Napoleon	16
National Swimming Society	93
naturism	69, 80-5, 88
Nelson, Horatio	21
New York Times	23
Nightingale, Florence	78
Nile, river	11
Norman Conquest	16
nude baptism, early Christians	42, 76
nudity, male Victorian perception of	68
nuns, morality bathing	42

O

Olympic Games	32, 71, 121, 130
Olympics, 1900 Paris	121
Onania	47
Oxford	16, 67, 91-2
ozone layer	89

P

package holidays, Spain	70
paddling pools	34, 92, 97-8, 100, 109, 132-3, 136, 140, 143
paedophiles	71, 82-4, 100, 150
Palm, Dr Adrian	78
Panathenaic Festival	75
paperboys, free swims Leicester	126
Parsons Pleasure, Oxford	16, 91
Paul, Apostle	40
peeping toms, seaside telescope	61
Penzance, Cornwall	110, 141
Peter Pan	94
Peter, apostle swimming?	40

Peterborough Lido	98
Phenolic disinfectant in hospitals	102
Philip, Dr Robin	106
photography and child protection	82-3
physicians recommend bathing	44
Picture Post	51
piers, seaside	22, 59
polio	101, 105, 112, 131
pollution	8, 108-9, 112, 131, 140
polo, water	23, 122, 142
Polruan, children swim harbour	104
Portreath, Cornwall	21
Post Bridge, Devon	113
postcards, saucy	61, 67, 81, 86, 88
Princess Alice, steamboat	26, 120
promenade at the seaside	59, 142
prostitutes and bathing	41, 45
prudery, British	26, 52, 54, 61, 72, 74, 82, 85-89, 112, 120, 138-9
Public Bath & Wash Houses Act	25
Public Health Act, 1875	80
public schools and swimming	30
pudenda, sex organs renamed	41
Punch, magazine	96

Q

quarries, swimming in	145-6, 150

R

rags as swimwear	68
Red Cross water safety program	32
Red Indians, American swimmers	22
religion, influence	39-40, 46, 48, 51, 53-4, 73, 86, 88, 96, 112, 116
rescue	24-5, 27-8, 30, 32, 99, 103, 109, 124, 137, 140, 147
resuscitation	25, 27
rickets	78-9, 98
river bathing	8, 11-3, 16, 18-9, 23-4, 26, 28, 30, 34-6, 42, 58, 63, 67-8, 77, 81, 90-2, 101-9, 112, 115-7, 119-144, 150-1
Robinson Crusoe (1719)	19
Rochdale canal, Manchester	108
Rollier, Dr	79
Romans	11-2, 14-6, 21, 30, 35-6, 41-43, 46, 75, 77, 112, 115, 138, 144
Rome	12-3, 16
Royal Humane Society	24-5, 27, 94-5
Royal Life Saving Society	27
rush floats, swimming aid	12, 115
Rutland Water, blue/green algae	132
rye grass, ergot and witchcraft	43

S

sanitation and health	40, 67, 101
sauna culture	72, 130
savages, lack of attire	19, 53, 78
Scandinavia, culture	72
Scarborough	18, 57, 62-3
Scott, Samuel	21
Scouts	28, 30, 49
sea bathing	20-1, 32, 51, 55, 57, 61, 63-4, 70, 78, 118, 140, 141
seawater as medicine	18
Serpentine, London	4, 24, 27, 93-7, 139, 143
sewage in rivers	26, 108
sex education	86, 88
Shakespeare, William	17
shame	39, 46, 53, 68, 72, 75-6, 85, 88, 117
Shanklin, Isle-of-White	64
shaving body hair for speed	71
Shulammite maiden, Bible	76
sidestroke	21
signs 'no swimming' danger of	124, 135
Skegness	69
skin cancer	71, 75, 89
skinny-dipping	67, 83, 94, 97
Slip-Slop-Slap campaign Australia	89
slum living conditions	52, 62, 85
Soar, river Leicester	140
solarium, Roman household	75
Southend-on-Sea	59
Southport	59
Spanish holidays	70
spas	15, 18-20, 42, 55, 57, 59, 61, 144
spectators, accommodation	98, 122, 130
Spence Street baths, Leicester	120
Spinney Hill Park, Leicester	124
St Clements, Oxford bathing place	91
St Ives, Cornwall	4, 142

Index

St Leonard's baths, Leicester 122
St Margaret's Baths, Leicester 130
steamboat, Princess Alice 25
Stoter, Mr Ted 96
Studland Nature Reserve 84
Sul, deity 14-5
sun cream 89
sun cure 79
sun lamps 80
sunbathing 36, 61, 69-70, 74-5, 78, 80-1, 84-5, 88-9, 97-8, 110, 112, 126-7, 139, 142-3, 146
Suren, Hans 80
Swainswick 14
swimming drills 31
Swimming Magazine (March 1884) 64
swimwear 8, 19, 55, 61, 63, 67-72, 78, 83-4, 91, 95, 97, 118, 120, 125, 138, 141, 150
Switzerland 72

T

Tarzan 32, 84
Teignmouth 33, 90
telescope at seaside 61
television effect on childrens activity 33, 83
tents, bathing 67
Thames, River 18-9, 24-6, 28, 31, 109, 120, 146
The Times 22
Tiber, River 12
Tidal pools 140
tin bath for bathing 67, 125
train, as holiday transport 57, 118
Travelling Light, naturist film 83
Trocadero, Leicester 128
tuberculosis 79, 98
Tuke, Henry Scott 66, 120
Tumbling Bay, Oxford 92
Turkish baths 22, 119
typhoid fever 129

U

underwear, bathing unnecessary 20

United Ladies Swimming Club, Leicester 125

V

vandalism at Lidos 99
vehicles, death by drowning 102
Venereal disease & bathing 45
verrucas 110
Vestry Street baths, Leicester 120
Victoria Park lake, London 7, 23, 26, 93, 129, 150
Victoria, Queen 52, 59, 118
Vikings 16
Visitor Book at seaside 59

W

walkers, death by drowning 102, 108
warm water swimming baths, Leicester 118
Warrilow, Mr Mark lido owner 128
Wash Houses Act 22
water quality, bathing waters 129, 132
water safety film 139
Waterlog, Roger Deakin 90, 144
Webb, Captain Matthew 23-4, 112, 119, 151
weeds, danger of entanglement 107, 135
Weil's disease 106-7, 124, 147
Weissmuller, Johnny 32
wells, holy 45, 55, 57
Welsh Harp Reservoir, Hendon, London 81
Weston-Super-Mare 100, 101
White House, USA, first bathroom 44
Whitgift, John, swimming restrictions 17
Windermere, Lake 24
windsurfer, first 23
witchcraft 43, 112
witches and water 43, 115
Wittie, Dr 18
Woodbridge, William 23
working class 22, 39, 46, 48, 52, 59-62, 66-7, 69-71, 85-8

Printed in Great Britain
by Amazon.co.uk, Ltd.,
Marston Gate.